Getting Started in Oral Interpretation

Getting Started in Oral Interpretation

Lanny Naegelin
North East Independent School District,
San Antonio, Texas

Ron Krikac
Bradley University, *Peoria, Illinois*

National Textbook Company
NTC a division of *NTC Publishing Group* • Lincolnwood, Illinois USA

Cover photos
Courtesy of North East Independent School District, San Antonio, Texas

Interior photos
North East Independent School District, San Antonio, Texas, pages 1, 9, 29, 57, 74, 87, 106
Jeff Ellis, pages 17, 47, 120

Published by National Textbook Company, a division of NTC Publishing Group.
©1993 by NTC Publishing Group, 4255 West Touhy Avenue,
Lincolnwood (Chicago), Illinois 60646-1975 U.S.A.
Library of Congress Catalog Card Number: 92–60577
Manufactured in the United States of America.

2 3 4 5 6 7 8 9 0 VP 9 8 7 6 5 4 3 2 1

Dedicated to my wife, my students, and all who love the art of interpretation!

—*Lanny Naegelin*

Dedicated to a special group of former students who have enriched my life with their continuing friendship and who have taught me their own versions of the ABCs of literature and life:

J.**A.**, E.**B.**, R.**C.**S., C.**D.**, **E.**G., N.**F.**, D.**G.**, D.**H.**Y., R.**I.**D., **J.**R., A.**K.**G., **L.**W., and **M.**M.

—*Ron Krikac*

Acknowledgments

Grateful acknowledgment is given to authors, publishers, and agents for permission to reprint the following copyrighted material. Every effort has been made to determine copyright owners. In the case of any omission, the publishers will be pleased to make suitable acknowledgment in future editions.

"My Mother Pieced Quilts" by Teresa Paloma Acosta from FESTIVAL DE FLOR Y CONTE. Originally published by University of Southern California Press. Reprinted by permission of El Centro Chicano, University of Southern California, Los Angeles.

Excerpt from I KNOW WHY THE CAGED BIRD SINGS by Maya Angelou. Copyright © 1969 by Maya Angelou. "Alone" from OH PRAY MY WINGS ARE GONNA FIT ME by Maya Angelou. Both are reprinted by permission of Random House, Inc.

"A Bug in Your Soup" by Jere Aston. Reprinted by permission of the author.

Excerpt from "The Ugliest Pilgrim" by Doris Betts from BEASTS OF THE SOUTHERN WILD AND OTHER STORIES, copyright © 1973 by Doris Betts. Reprinted by permission of Russell & Volkening as agents for the author.

Excerpts from WHEN THE LEGENDS DIE by Hal Borland. Copright © 1963 by Hal Borland. Reprinted by permission of HarperCollins Publishers.

Excerpts from THE GOOD EARTH by Pearl Buck. Copyright 1931 by Pearl S. Buck. Reprinted by permission of HarperCollins Publishers.

"Sea Gull" from SUMMER GREEN by Elizabeth Coatsworth. Copyright 1947 by Macmillan Publishing, renewed 1975 by Elizabeth Coatsworth Beston.

Excerpt from THE GREAT SANTINI by Pat Conroy. Copyright © 1976 by Pat Conroy. Reprinted by permission of Houghton Mifflin Co. All rights reserved.

"Winter" by William Dean, reprinted by permission of the author.

Excerpt from A YOUNG LADY OF PROPERTY by Horton Foote. © 1955 by Horton Foote. All inquiries (except for amateur rights) should be addressed to the author's representative, Lucy Kroll Agency, 390 West End Ave., Suite 9B, New York, New York 10024. The amateur acting rights are controlled by Dramatists' Play Service, Inc., 440 Park Ave. South, New York, New York 10019.

"The Runaway" from THE POETRY OF ROBERT FROST edited by Edward Connery Lathem. Copyright 1923, © 1969 by Holt, Rinehart and Winston. Copyright 1951 by Robert Frost. Reprinted by permission of Henry Holt and Company, Inc.

Excerpt from THE BIG RIVER by William Hauptman. Copyright © 1986 by William Hauptman. Used by permission of Grove Press, Inc.

"Lover's Toy" by Janell Howard from EACH HAS SPOKEN © 1974. Reprinted by permission of the author.

"Deer Hunt" by Judson Jerome. Reprinted by permission of The Golden Quill Press, New Hampshire.

"The Creation" from GOD'S TROMBONES by James Weldon Johnson. Copyright 1927 The Viking Press, Inc., © renewed 1955 by Grace Nail Johnson. Used by permission of Viking Penguin, a division of Penguin Books USA Inc.

"Freddy" by Dennis Lee, © 1981 Dennis Lee.

Excerpt from TO KILL A MOCKINGBIRD by Harper Lee. © 1960 by Harper Lee. Reprinted by permission of HarperCollins Publishers Inc.

Excerpt from "Skating Song" in THE MOON AND A STAR AND OTHER POEMS by Myra Cohn Livingston. © 1965 by Myra Cohn Livingston. Reprinted by permission of Marian Reiner for the author.

"We're Racing, Racing ..." by Phyllis McGinley. Reprinted by permission of Curtis Brown Ltd. Copyright © 1959, 1960 by Phyllis McGinley. Renewed 1987, 1988.

Acknowledgments

Contents

Chapter 1   Discovering Interpretation   1

The Process of Interpreting Literature 2

The First Step into Interpretation: Analysis 2

The Second Step into Interpretation: Performance 6

Chapter 2   Speaking with Your Body and Voice   9

Teaching Your Body to Speak 9

Teaching Your Voice to Have Body 13

Chapter 3   Analyzing Prose   17

Prose, A Definition 17

Plot: What's Going on Here? 18

Setting: Where Are We? 19

Characters: Who's Involved? 19

The Narrator: Who's In Charge Here? 21

Point of View: Do You See What I See? 25

Identifying Point of View 27

Chapter 4 Prose, from Printed Page to Performance 29

A Story to Study 29

Knowing the Narrator 34

Staging the Setting 37

Dealing with Dialogue 37

Tasteful Trimming 38

Miscellaneous Matters 39

Preparing for Presentation 39

Chapter 5 Analyzing Poetry 47

Poetry, A Definition 48

Rockin' Rhythm 48

Time for Rhyme 52

Other Sound Harmonies 54

The Connection of Meaning and Sound 55

Chapter 6 Poetry, from Printed Page to Performance 57

Figures of Speech 58

Types of Poetry 60

Putting the Preparation Process to Work 61

Introducing the Interpretation 64

Exploring Options for Performance 65

Bringing Poetry to Life 66

Chapter 7 Analyzing Drama 74

Sensing the Structure 75

Concentrating on Conflict 75

A Play to Probe 76

Combing the Content   81

Succeeding with the Subtext   82

Regarding Relationships   84

Acting and Interpretation   86

Chapter 8   Drama, from Printed Page to Performance   87

Getting Physical   87

Dealing with Details   90

Finding the Focus   91

Establishing the Environment   92

Plotting the Progression   94

Cutting, Dialect, and the Sound of Silence   95

Concentrating on Commitment   96

Chapter 9   Group Interpretation   106

Reading Together   106

Creating the Ensemble Effect   107

Group and Duo Interpretation   112

Chapter 10   Rehearsal and Evaluation   120

Rehearsing as Part of the Overall Process   120

Evaluating Your Own Performance   122

Becoming an Effective Critic   124

A Final Word   128

Glossary of Key Terms   129

Index of Literary Selections and Authors   131

1 Discovering Interpretation

Journey to the Past . . .

Imagine yourself living thousands of years ago— long before the invention of television, motion pictures, radio, or even books, a time before written language had developed. Even then people found pleasure in telling others about important events in their lives. Perhaps a hunter would relate to his spellbound listeners the way he cleverly stalked and killed a wild boar in the brush. Perhaps a young girl would tell her friends the frightening tale of her narrow escape from the angry bear she met while gathering berries in the woods. Or perhaps an ancient leader of the tribe would recount the adventures of a band of warriors who long ago had heroically defended their tribe against attackers from another area. In these stories, no doubt told with great emotion and even acted out at times, was born the art known today as interpretation.

The enjoyment of a good story is a universal pleasure. Everyone enjoys an exciting, moving, or humorous episode told by a master storyteller. And the amount of pleasure listeners get from hearing such tales is closely related to the skill of the storyteller in making the action and characters so vivid that everyone in the audience is drawn in and comes to understand and share the experience being narrated.

Eventually the best stories become the myths or history of a group of people, common tales that bind a group together to form their unique culture. Thus literature develops out of a need to share common life experiences, to understand what it means to live a human existence, and to create thrills, suspense, and drama.

Oral interpretation is a specialized way of studying literature. The interpreter makes an intensive exploration of a literary work and then conveys to the audience his or her total intellectual, emotional, spiritual, and physical understanding of the work by performing it.

The Process of Interpreting Literature

The art of interpretation involves two important steps: the first is mainly an activity of the mind as you explore the work you will perform; the second is the act of performance by which you use your body and voice to convey what you have discovered during your careful exploration.

Because the interpreter studies the chosen literary work in great detail to be able to perform it convincingly and believably, it is important to select material of good quality. A work that is too simple or too poorly written will impose unnecessary limitations. The best literature will provide a good mental challenge as well as a rich opportunity for an exciting performance.

How will you recognize good literature? One characteristic of quality literature is universality. That is, it deals with some aspect of human life that is common to all people, no matter in what time period they live or from what culture they come. Honest and sensitive treatment of such universalities as human relationships, great achievements, love, courage, death, and adventure appeal to most people because these experiences are part of life.

At the same time, good literature treats these subjects or themes with originality. The best authors try to make their readers see a human experience from a new angle or understand it in a different way. In order to make their works fresh and unique, they avoid overused plots, stereotypical characters, and clichéd expressions.

Sometimes it is difficult for beginning interpreters to recognize outstanding literature as they have not had many years of reading experience. For this reason it is often wise to ask your teacher for guidance in picking suitable literature for performance. After you have worked with interpretation for a time, you will gain the ability to choose appropriate literature that lends itself to exciting performance.

It is also important to perform material that you genuinely like, literature that affects you deeply and that you want to share with others. At the same time, it's good to explore some literature that you may not be immediately drawn to. Much good literature does not reveal its rewards on first reading. Some of the best stories, poems, and plays unfold their treasures only after you spend considerable time with them. It's good to explore such works, for your experiences with them will broaden your horizons and increase your understanding of human experiences.

Activity 1   Recalling and Sharing

1. Recall a story, poem, or play that you have read recently. What common experience or experiences did the work of literature share?
2. What insights about human existence came to you as a result of reading this particular literary work?
3. Point out elements of suspense or drama that were part of the work.
4. Did the work have the necessary elements to make it a good selection to perform for an audience? Explain your response. ■

The First Step into Interpretation: Analysis

The first step in preparing a work for performance is **analysis,** a studied exploration of the literature that begins when you read the selection aloud several times in order to get a general understanding. Oral interpretation teacher Wallace Bacon has referred to this step as "letting the text speak to you." Charlotte Lee, another expert in the field, advises, "Let the material work on you before you begin to work on it." In this way you get an intuitive feeling for the entire selection before you begin to examine its complex parts.

Next, search the text for any words whose meanings are not absolutely clear to you. It's not enough to have a vague or general idea of what a word means. Good authors choose words that convey specific meanings they want to communicate. Without knowing these meanings yourself, you will be unable to transmit them to an audience.

Unfortunately, misunderstanding even a single word can sometimes lead the performer to a distorted interpretation. A student once read Edgar Lee Masters' poem "Enoch Dunlap" in a way that made Enoch appear to feel warm and kindly toward the audience he is addressing. Yet Dunlap calls these people "common rabble," an indication that he thinks them a loud, crude, disorderly mob. Because the interpreter erroneously believed the word *rabble* meant people Dunlap respected and admired, he grossly misinterpreted the poem.

Good interpreters understand more than the literal or dictionary definition of a word, its **denotative meaning:** they understand that a word may also have various attitudes and associations connected with it, its **connotative meaning.** For example, the words *female, woman,* and *lady* may sometimes be synonyms; but the words have very different connotations. In using the word *female,* a writer suggests a scientific attitude, a reference to such a being in a biological classification. The word *woman* suggests a human adult of non-male gender. *Lady,* sometimes considered a sexist term, can also suggest that the person has a certain refinement and perhaps even a high social rank. As an interpreter, you must be sensitive to a word's connotative meanings so that you can color the word in just the right way to convey the author's intended meaning.

It's also important for you to pay attention to the title an author gives a work, for that title can help you to understand aspects of the work that might otherwise escape you. In William Mastrosimone's play *The Woolgatherer,* for instance, a reader might assume the plot concerns someone who collects and processes sheep's fleece. But a less familiar definition of *woolgatherer* is a daydreamer, a person who engages in purposeless fantasies. This is the definition that is more helpful in understanding the play, for it emphasizes the pastime of one of the main characters. In addition, the character Rose collects or *gathers* wool sweaters from people she encounters so she'll have something by which to remember them. Like many titles, *The Woolgatherer* has several levels of meaning, all of which help the reader to understand the complexities of the work.

Be certain to check the pronunciation of unfamiliar words. Readers who mispronounce words embarrass themselves and make their audiences question how well the performers prepared or understood the work.

Once you have read the work aloud to get a feel for it and looked up all the unfamiliar words, you are ready to begin a more intensive exploration of the selection.

It is now necessary to consider who is speaking the words, whom the speaker is addressing, and why the interchange is taking place. Once you have answered these questions, you will have a strong foundation on which to build your performance. As a beginning interpreter working to master the fundamentals of oral performance, you will find that material with a clearly defined speaker, persona, or narrator will serve you well.

In plays it is easy to see who is speaking particular lines. However, the idea that there is an implied speaker in most nondramatic works may be new to you. It is a helpful concept to explore. In considering the question of who is speaking the words in a prose or poetry selection, you may at first think the author is speaking; but that is not a safe assumption to make. True, sometimes the speaker seems very much like the author, but other times the speaker and author are not even the same gender. Authors often step outside themselves as they spin their tales or share feelings. For this reason, it's probably better to think of the speaker as someone other than the author. Then it becomes your task to discover who the speaker is.

The implied speaker in a poem is called the **persona.** In a work of prose fiction, the speaker is called the **narrator.** Sometimes it's easy to discover who the persona or narrator is. In Edgar Lee Masters' *Spoon River Anthology,* for example, the author names the speaker of each poem. Each individual returns from the dead to make a statement about his or her life. Masters also makes clear in these small sketches what kinds of personalities these people possess. Examine his poem "Lucinda Matlock" to see what information he reveals about her.

> I went to dances at Chandlerville,
> And played snap-out at Winchester.
> One time we changed partners,
> Driving home in the moonlight of middle June,
> And then I found Davis.
> We were married and lived together for seventy years,
> Enjoying, working, raising the twelve children,
> Eight of whom we lost
> Ere I had reached the age of sixty.
> I spun, I wove, I kept the house, I nursed the sick,
> I made the garden, and for holiday
> Rambled over the fields where sang the larks,
> And by Spoon River gathering many a shell,
> And many a flower and medicinal weed—
> Shouting to the wooded hills, singing to the green valleys.
> At ninety-six I had lived enough, that is all,
> And passed to a sweet repose.
> What is this I hear of sorrow and weariness,
> Anger, discontent and drooping hopes?
> Degenerate sons and daughters,
> Life is too strong for you—
> It takes life to love Life.

Through Masters' word portrait of Lucinda you learn, among other things, that she died at ninety-six, apparently her age when she speaks the poem's words; that she had married Davis and given birth to twelve children; that she remained energetic and happy all her life; and that she considers the younger generation somewhat weak. As a performer of the poem, your job is to embody Lucinda's qualities, to make her alive and real for your audience.

The listeners in this poem are indicated when Lucinda speaks directly to the "degenerate sons and daughters" of a later generation. In many poems, however, the listeners are not named. Instead, they are only implied. As you analyze the work, you must decide, in light of the information the author provides, to whom the persona or narrator might be speaking the lines. Often there is no absolutely right answer to the question. As the interpreter, you must make a choice among the various options you find. Some possibilities for the implied listener include the speaker's friend or confidante, a clergyman, a loved one or relative, a psychiatrist, or a passerby. Sometimes it is even possible that the speaker in a poem or story is talking to himself or herself, perhaps rehearsing what might be said to a friend or relative. Be careful of deciding too quickly that the person is speaking to himself or herself. Explore a wide selection of reasonable options and choose the one that will help you create the most exciting performance.

Finally, even though the work may provide no obvious answer, you need to consider *why* the persona or narrator is speaking. In real life people rarely speak to others just to hear their own voices. Rather they have a purpose or **intention.** They want to influence their listeners to *do* something. Usually, the stronger the desire to get the listener to act, the stronger will be the intensity of the speaker. What is Lucinda Matlock attempting to get her listeners, the "degenerate sons and daughters," to do? Is she urging them to reexamine their easy lives by teasingly referring to them as degenerate? The decision you make concerning how she feels about these people and what she wants them to do will color her whole speech because she begins the speech knowing the points she wants to make. In other words, she knows her intention, her goal. As the interpreter, you must know the speaker's intention and make it clear throughout your performance.

Once you have thought out the answers to these questions and other more specific matters discussed in the chapters dealing specifically with the interpretation of poetry, prose, and drama, you will be ready to move to the second stage—the rehearsal of your performance.

Activity 2   Exploring a Text

1. Here are two more poems from Edgar Lee Masters' *Spoon River Anthology.* Each deals with the same incident as seen through the eyes of a different persona. Read the two poems until you have a clear understanding of each one. Look up any words you don't know.

Knowlt Hoheimer

I was the first fruits of the battle of Missionary Ridge.*
When I felt the bullet enter my heart
I wished I had staid at home and gone to jail
For stealing the hogs of Curl Trenary,
Instead of running away and joining the army.
Rather a thousand times the county jail
Than to lie under this marble figure with wings,
And this granite pedestal
Bearing the words, *"Pro Patria."*
What do they mean, anyway?

Lydia Puckett

Knowlt Hoheimer ran away to the war
The day before Curl Trenary
Swore out a warrant through Justice Arnett
For stealing hogs.
But that's not the reason he turned a soldier.
He caught me running with Lucius Atherton.**
We quarreled and I told him never again
To cross my path.
Then he stole the hogs and went to the war—
Back of every soldier is a woman.

2. How well educated is Knowlt? You might consider his spelling of the word *staid* and his inability to understand the meaning of *Pro Patria* ("for one's country" in Latin). How well educated is Lydia? How would their educational levels affect the way they speak?

---

* Missionary Ridge: An important Civil War battle fought on November 25, 1863, near Chattanooga, Tennessee.

** Lucius Atherton: Atherton was a resident of Spoon River, and a subject of another of Masters' poems. As a youth he was a romantic man-about-town who frequently broke young girls' hearts.

3. What do you think Knowlt's life has been like? Why do you believe he stole the hogs?

4. Do you believe Lydia is giving a true account of Knowlt's real reason for going to war? Does Lydia believe the story she tells? Defend your answers.

5. How does Lydia feel about herself? Does she think she's an important person? Do you detect a streak of romanticism in her? If so, has it influenced her sense of reality?

6. To whom do you think each character is speaking? What is the intention each has in speaking?

7. How does Knowlt feel about Curl Trenary? the hogs? running away to join the army? going to jail? the monument above him?

8. How does Lydia feel about the war? Knowlt's death? Knowlt's theft of the hogs? Lucius Atherton? herself? ∎

The Second Step into Interpretation: Performance

Once you have analyzed a work and are confident that you have a basic understanding of it, you are ready to move to the second stage: performance. In this part of your preparation, you begin to put into practice the discoveries you made in your analysis. You may be surprised to discover, however, that as you repeatedly read the work aloud, you will gain further insights into the way a piece of good literature works. Even after you have rehearsed a selection many times, you may find that in performing it for an audience you become aware of new, exciting aspects of the poem, story, or play that you had not seen before. So you can see that analysis and performance are not entirely separate activities: your performance will enable you to understand aspects of the work that eluded you in analysis just as the careful analysis has enabled you to understand aspects of the work that might have eluded you if you had prepared the performance only by reading the selection aloud.

Your task as a performer is to **embody** the work you present for an audience. In a way you lend your body to the speaker in the literature and let that character speak through you. If that sounds like a rather mystical experience, it is! A good reader, like an actor, allows himself or herself to become so deeply involved in the experience that he or she may seem almost possessed. Of course, the oral reader remains in control of voice and body; but a good performer conceals technique so well that the audience members can become enthralled by the experience being shared and forget they are watching a student performance. **It is the goal of every performance to convince the audience of the reality of the experience or situation being shared by the interpreter.**

Although the specific challenges of performing poetry, prose, and drama will be considered in later chapters, at this point you can begin to consider some of the challenges common to all genres.

One problem or challenge you as an interpreter will confront is how to suggest a persona, narrator, or character whose age is different from your own. Usually, especially in the interpretation of drama, you cannot avoid portraying at least one character who is older, often considerably older, than you. How can you be convincing in such a situation?

The answer is that you need not assume such a full physical characterization as an actor might; rather, your job as an interpreter is to *suggest* the essential qualities of the person. If you are successful in capturing the essence of the character's age, you can count on your audience's imagination to complete the illusion.

Begin your task with observation: go to a spot where you can unobtrusively watch many people of the age you want to portray. A shopping mall is a good place to go; but other places also offer rich opportunities; for example, a restaurant, a church, a park, a sports event, a musical or theatrical performance. One of the first things you will probably notice is the great variety of people of the same age. There is no such thing as a typical person. A common mistake young performers make is to portray everyone over the age of fifty or sixty as ancient, senile physical ruins. That's hardly a reasonable generalization! Some older people may be physically impaired; but there are also vigorous ninety-year-olds whose daily activities may include swimming, bicycling, and jogging. When preparing to portray any character, think in terms of the specific qualities that person may possess. Don't play an attitude or strike a pose. Create a characterization that is unique and honest.

In physicalizing a character, you will find certain qualities common to particular age groups. Young people generally have bounce and agility. As people grow older, they tend to shift the way they carry their weight. They may rest it more on the middle or back of their feet than on their toes. As people become less sure of bodily strength and balance, they generally take smaller, more cautious steps; they reduce the size and energy of their movements; and they have difficulty maintaining erect posture. By using these observations as guides, you can adjust your body to suggest relative degrees of aging without going to extremes.

The voice, too, changes as human beings age. If you listen carefully to the speech of elderly people, you will find that not all of them have cracked voices and high pitches. Rather, age tends to limit the inflections of the voice, slow the rate of speaking, and reduce the energy level. Again, there are as many voices as there are people. You must determine appropriate voices for the personalities the author has created and adjust your own voice accordingly to suggest believably the ages of the characters you portray.

Another special challenge you will face is how to portray a character of the opposite sex. This is an especially delicate problem because if you inaccurately portray someone of the opposite gender, you may seem unintentionally comic or disrespectful and thus limit your effectiveness or even ruin an otherwise good performance.

Again, suggestion is the key to a convincing portrayal. You do not want to make exaggerated changes in posture, bodily tension, and voice to create a person of the opposite sex. Rather a few subtle changes are all that will be necessary. This matter is especially critical to the performance of drama.

By observation, you will notice that men generally stand with their feet about shoulder width apart and their weight to the center or back of their feet. Women, on the other hand, often stand with their feet closer together and their weight slightly forward. Men tend to make broad, firm movements when they gesture, whereas women generally use light, fluid movements. Of course, close observation of men's and women's actions will show you the great variety of possibilities open to you. You must be careful not to rely on stereotypes. Instead, create individualized characters consistent with the qualities the author has specified or implied.

Adjustments in the voice must be subtle. Performers who force their voices as low as possible for men and as high as possible for women will strain their vocal cords and limit their flexibility and believability. Any adjustment in pitch should be slight. Clear changes in vocal quality are a better way to suggest the opposite gender. A woman needs only to take deeper breaths, relax her throat, and speak with a little greater force to suggest a man; a man can lighten his vocal quality, use more breath, and reduce his projection to suggest a woman. He should not use a forced falsetto voice as that will certainly be unconvincing and comic. Using such a voice should be avoided even for humorous characters unless something in the personality of the character calls for such a quality.

Activity 3 Making Decisions

1. Look at the poems "Knowlt Hoheimer" and "Lydia Puckett." Assuming they speak to the listeners at the age they died, how old do you think Knowlt and Lydia are? What hints lead you to your conclusions?

2. How would you describe Knowlt? How would you describe Lydia? What might you do to suggest each of these characters vocally and physically?

3. Look at the poem "Lucinda Matlock." What kind of voice would you use to suggest her age and character? What might you do to suggest her character physically?

4. Find your own poem or short prose selection in which the persona or narrator seems to speak directly to the audience. Analyze the speaker completely. What are his or her age, background, and personal characteristics? Why is the person telling the story? How would you go about creating that speaker vocally and physically? Why did you arrive at the decisions you made? Be prepared to read at least one minute of the selection to demonstrate how you might translate your mental decisions about character into actual performance. ■

2 Speaking with Your Body and Voice

Consider the Possibility . . .

You have been selected as an Olympic athlete to compete in the decathlon, that grueling contest in which you must excel in ten demanding events to win the gold medal. What would you do to prepare for such a challenge? A little research would show you that past winners have been athletes who developed the best all-around skills and conditioning of the body, the ones who coordinated their breathing to give themselves maximum power and energy, the ones who had the best total preparation. More than any other athlete, the decathlon champion must have a human instrument disciplined to do everything demanded of it.

The interpreter is in a way like that versatile athlete, for the most successful performer will be the one whose body and voice can fulfill every demand made of them. In the previous chapter you learned that as an interpreter you may be asked to embody characters of all ages, of both genders, of various physical types, and of wide-ranging emotions. To do so, you must possess a flexible and controlled body and voice that have the strength and endurance to sustain an energized performance. Now you will explore some of the ways of developing such a versatile human instrument. Because the human voice and body are so closely interrelated, it is hard to discuss them separately; however, because the body's conditioning is the foundation for vocal production, a discussion of the body is the best place to begin.

Teaching Your Body to Speak

The first thing your audience will notice about you is your body: even before you say a word, they will observe your posture, your energy level, the ease with which you move, and even the amount of tension you carry. Through these aspects and more, your body will convey to the audience a certain attitude, and they will begin to respond to that attitude almost immediately. In fact, studies show that your audience will have formed a strong first impression of you within ten seconds of seeing you! For this reason it is important that you seem relaxed, confident, and sincere. In this way you can make the audience feel comfortable and thus ready to receive the literature you are about to share.

Activity 1 Observing and Testing Postures

1. Observe three of your classmates as they appear before you: one standing in a slouched position with his or her weight shifted to one foot; the second standing stiffly as if at attention with head held very high, legs locked, and arms held tightly to the sides of the body; the third standing comfortably with his or her weight balanced on the balls of both feet, the chest and head held up, the posture erect but relaxed, and the arms hanging comfortably at the sides. Which of these three people would you prefer to watch and listen to? What message does each of these stances convey to the audience? Which person will make the strongest first impression on the audience?

2. Now you stand in each of the positions described. How does each position make you feel? Which position would be the best for you to use in performing for an audience? What do you gain from standing in that position? What do you lose from standing in either of the other two positions? ■

As a performer, you can communicate a great deal merely through your posture. It is important that you have a relaxed, comfortable, neutral position when you first appear before your audience. You will find that the various adjustments of the body to suggest the characters being portrayed will flow most easily from such a position.

There is another important reason that you must feel relaxed and comfortable: unnecessary tension in your body will cause a certain stiffness and awkwardness in movement and a less flexible and less pleasant sounding voice. At the same time, when you eliminate tension you must not lose your energy. As you gain experience in performing, you will learn to find that happy balance between relaxation and energy that is sometimes called **controlled relaxation.**

Activity 2 Stretching and Loosening Muscles

1. Pretend that you have just awakened for the morning. Lift your arms above your head and make your fingers and arms as long as possible. Rise on your toes as you reach as high as you can. Feel your back, neck, legs, and arms S - T - R - E - T - C - H. Then slowly relax into a normal standing position.

2. Lie on your back on the floor. Slowly raise your knees and swing them up to your chest. Wrap your arms tightly around your legs and pull them into your chest. Raise your head and gently rock back and forth. Can you feel your back and neck stretching? Be careful not to strain. Just allow yourself to lengthen your back and neck. Now slowly return to your original position.

3. Before attempting this exercise, remove your eyeglasses, loose jewelry, or pocket items that might scatter. Begin by gently shaking your hands, keeping the wrists and finger joints as loose as you can. After about ten seconds, extend the looseness to the elbow and finally to the shoulders. Loosen the neck and let the head move freely as you continue to shake the hands and arms. Be certain to keep the elbow and shoulders loose: don't be too sharp in your movements. After a few seconds, stop and feel the tingling sensations in your hands and arms.

4. Now, one leg at a time, do similar shake-outs, starting with the ankle and gradually adding the knee and the hip. Again be careful not to be too violent in your actions. None of this action should hurt in any way.

5. Finally let the whole body go into a kind of frenzied dance that shakes the tension out of the joints and makes all your muscles feel loose and relaxed. After a few seconds of such activity, stop and stand in a comfortable stance. Not only will your major muscles be freed of tension, but you will probably find that you feel greatly energized as well. ■

Grounded in an energetic but relaxed physical stance, you are prepared to use your body to communicate all that the literature demands, all that is required to suggest the characters' physical and emotional responses. Sometimes a response is very subtle—a shift in body tension, a glance, a shrug of the shoulders; other times the response may be stronger—a sharp toss of the head, a grimace, or a broad gesture of the hand or arm. It is important that the response is appropriate, that it communicates clearly, and that it does not call attention to itself by being extreme or awkward.

Activity 3 Responding from Head to Toe

1. Say each of the following lines. Let your body respond fully from head to toe. Don't exaggerate or force yourself to react unnaturally. Instead, imagine yourself in a situation or scene where these lines might be expressed, and let the line tell your body how to respond.

   - Look out! That beam is falling!
   - I couldn't care less.
   - This chocolate ice cream tastes s-o-o-o good.
   - I did it. I'm the world champion!
   - Who cares?
   - What is that awful smell?
   - What can I say?
   - You do that again, and I'll smash your ugly face!
   - I'm so tired I'm going to sleep for a week.
   - Shhh! Listen! Can you hear that faint humming sound?

2. How did your body tension change as you said each of these lines? How did your face respond? What kinds of movements or gestures did your body make as you spoke? Did you listen, taste, smell, see, and feel with your whole body? If not, try the lines again while imagining a different situation. Repeat the exercise until you can feel yourself responding from head to toe on each line. ■

The way your body responds to the material you read is very important because your body communicates to the audience the way *they* should respond to what they are hearing. Just as you identify with the speaker or narrator of a piece of literature and respond physically and emotionally to that person's situation, so does the audience respond to you. This ability human beings have to share such experience or to feel with another person is called **empathy,** and it is essential for both the performer and the audience.

Have you watched avid wrestling fans during a close match? Did you notice how their bodies begin to move and respond to the situation of the wrestler they're encouraging? The more involved they become, the more their body positions and tension match those of the wrestler. At the end of the match, they may feel as tired—and as elated or depressed—as the athlete who competed on the mat! This **empathic response** is the same kind the interpreter wants to achieve. Performers respond empathically—physically and emotionally—to the events created in the literature; the audience in turn responds physically and emotionally to the performers. When the performers are totally involved in the experiences they are embodying and the audience is likewise involved, the performance has a sense of electricity. It becomes exciting!

It is obvious, then, that to become a good performer you must be able to respond fully to the material you present. You must remember the feeling of an experience—or at least imagine it—in order to communicate the sensations through the body and the voice so that the audience members may share that experience.

Activity 4   Making Your Muscles Remember

1. Using a sturdy piece of rope about eight feet long, have a tug-of-war with a partner. Notice how the rope feels in your hands; how your feet dig in so that you won't slip; how your knees bend and the muscles of your upper arms tense; how you breathe— or don't breathe; how you set your teeth, distribute your weight, and watch your opponent in anticipation of the moves he or she might make. Struggle to win for at least one minute.

2. After a short rest, repeat the tug-of-war, this time without the rope. Watch your partner intently so that you can react to his or her mistakes. Remember the feel of the rope, the muscle tension, the way you held your breath, the way you set your teeth and distributed your weight. Try to make this pantomimed reenactment as realistic as the contest with the real rope. After a minute, end the struggle and discuss with your partner how your body feels.

3. Now read the following passage and let your entire body respond to the events. You won't act out the story this time. It's in the past tense, and the narrator is remembering the event and telling about it, not reenacting it. As you read, let your muscles remember how the tug-of-war felt, and let your body naturally tense and relax in response to the ebb and flow of the tensions suggested by the words. Make the story so vivid that your audience can sense your physical remembrance and respond with you. Make them feel the heat, smell the odors, taste the salt.

THE TUG-OF-WAR STORY

As Chris grasped the thick yellow rope, he looked across the dark circle on the gymnasium floor to the face of his opponent, Roger Dablow. Twice before these two had met in this arena, and Roger had won both matches. Tonight he was confident—even cocky—as he grinned at his shorter opponent. Chris wrapped the rope tightly around his right hand, feeling the coarse fibers dig into his palm. Testing the grip of his shoes against the floor, he planted his right foot ahead of his left and flexed his knees. He could feel the rope tense as Roger positioned himself across the circle.

The heat oppressed him, and he felt a bead of sweat run down his forehead and drop onto his upper lip. He tasted its warm saltiness. The acrid odor of stale perspiration and the tightness of his stomach combined to make him feel a little sick. He swallowed hard and gritted his teeth as the referee raised his arms to signal "Ready." A quick breath, a flash from a camera, "Go!"

Roger was quick. His long legs gave leverage, and Chris felt his arms jerk forward. He set his feet and fell back instinctively against the pull. Now both boys braced, and the resulting tension held them immobile, frozen. Silence. Stretch. Silence. Already Chris's upper arm ached with the strain, and his eyes throbbed, feeling ready to rupture. He knew Roger's endurance; he had to jerk, to pull him off balance, and then hurl himself backward and grab control. He needed air, a deep breath, but he dared not exhale. Lungs full, throat tight, heart pounding, he strained against the pull of his heavier opponent. "One," he counted, pressing the side of his shoe into the floor; "two," he thought as he caught a quick breath; "three!" He arched his body backward and felt a surge of strength. Roger slid forward, slightly off balance. "Yes!"

Desperate, Chris grabbed a breath and hurled himself backward again, twisting his body to gain another precious inch.

4. Your next assignment is to evaluate what you did. Did your muscles remember your tug-of-war and your pantomimed tug-of-war as you read the story? Did you feel your muscles tense and relax in response to the events of the story? Were your responses natural and yet strong enough that an audience could perceive them and respond to them? Did you notice how the verbs especially suggested the different levels of tension?

5. Find a short poem or a paragraph from a short story or a novel that expresses some action sequence that is familiar to you, one that your muscles have experienced. Try to find a selection with strong, vivid verbs. The material, when read, should run about one or two minutes. Using what you have learned about physical response, prepare to read the selection aloud to a partner or to your class. ■

Teaching Your Voice to Have Body

As you develop your performance skills, you will not want to neglect your voice. A strong and flexible vocal instrument is essential to create a variety of believable characters as well as to communicate the subtle variations of emotion in the literature. As was mentioned earlier, good vocal production is dependent upon a relaxed and responsive body that allows you to breathe correctly.

Often students are surprised to learn that there are correct and incorrect methods of breathing. They assume that breathing is just a natural process. And it is—at least it starts out that way.

A baby breathes easily and naturally from the abdomen. If you watch a baby, you will see that as the child breathes there is a regular expansion and contraction of the lower rib cage and abdomen. As a person grows older, however, the activities and pressures of the world bring more tensions to the body. This tension influences breathing by restricting bodily movement. The result is a more shallow breathing that doesn't carry the air deep into the abdomen. You may observe that many of your fellow students as well as many adults often raise and lower their shoulders slightly as they breathe, a sign that they are not breathing correctly.

Breath is the foundation of everything people do and say. If your breathing is restricted, your voice will be too. Without proper breathing and support, your voice will lack power, vocal range, quality, and flexibility.

So how can you check to see if you have proper breathing habits? If you do have them, how can you strengthen your breath control? If you lack them, how can you go about developing good breathing technique? Activity 5 will help you answer each of these questions.

Activity 5　Breathing Properly

1. To begin, stand before a mirror and take several deep breaths. Did you feel and see your abdomen expand? Did your shoulders move?

2. Remain standing comfortably erect and place your hands, palms toward you, in the small of your back. Allow the middle fingers of your hands barely to touch each other. Now take a deep, full breath and imagine expanding your chest as if it were a large bag filling with water. Do you feel your lower back widening? Do your fingers move slightly apart? They should if you are breathing correctly.

3. Next, lie on your back on the floor. Relax and let your shoulders touch the surface. Close your eyes and breathe in, *inhale,* deeply. Can you feel the breath filling the abdomen? Hold the breath for about three seconds and then let it go, *exhale.* Could you feel your abdomen collapse? Repeat the exercise three or four times until you feel fully at ease.

4. Remain where you are; but now as you exhale, let out a sigh with the breath. Keeping an open throat, continue to breathe and exhale with that sound. Let yourself relax as you continue to inhale fully and then exhale with the sigh. ■

Vocal sound is produced in the larynx, commonly called the Adam's apple or voice box. Within it are two folds of muscle, the vocal cords, which are set into motion by air exhaled from the lungs. Their vibrations generate the sounds that eventually you shape into words. In order for these words to come out clearly and resonantly, it is important to keep the throat relaxed and open. Tension in the throat can hurt your voice quality and limit the range of pitches or tones your voice can produce. Worse, continued misuse of your voice by creating excessive tension and forcing unusual sounds can do permanent damage. Properly used, your voice can accomplish an amazing variety of sounds; but any vocal production that causes pain or hoarseness should be stopped. Consult your teacher if you suspect any problems.

Activity 6　Phonating Sound

1. Repeat steps 3 and 4 of the previous activity, but instead of exhaling with a sigh, count aloud at a normal speaking rate. Do not "squeeze" out more numbers than you can comfortably say. Stop counting when speaking becomes difficult. How far did you get? Try again. Attempt to reach the number 60, a sign that you have good breath control.

2. Now stand up and, breathing the same way, repeat the counting exercise. Try this routine every day until you can comfortably reach 60 every time. When you are habitually breathing correctly, you will have provided a solid foundation for your voice. ■

The sound produced by the vibration of your vocal cords is soft and thin. It becomes enriched and strengthened by the resonators in your head, much the same way a tuning fork's sound becomes louder and richer when the fork touches a hollow wooden box called a resonance chamber. Your vocal sound is amplified and modified by your throat, your mouth, your nasal cavities, and even the sinus cavities in the front of your face. By placing your voice forward to take advantage of these resonating cavities, you can develop a rich, full voice capable of producing an almost infinite number of vocal qualities.* Such qualities enable

---

* The term *quality* or *timbre* refers to a particular attribute or coloring of a voice that makes it distinguishable from others. Each person has his or her own unique quality. That's why you can easily recognize other people's voices on the telephone. If you are familiar with musical instruments, you may know that a violin, a trombone, and a piano can all produce middle C. But the listener has no trouble telling which instrument is playing because each has its distinct quality of sound.

you to communicate subtle shades of emotion as well as to distinguish the voices of extremely different characters.

One important outcome of this forward placement is that it will enable you to create mature-sounding character voices without strain. Many young performers try to get the "older" sound by forcing the voice down in pitch and placing it back in the throat. Because doing so produces an unnatural sound that can create damaging tension in the throat, it's important for you to master proper placement.

Activity 7   Resonating Sound

1. Stand comfortably erect with your weight balanced on the balls of both feet. Now Y-A-W-N! Let this be a BIG yawn that opens and relaxes the throat. Make a sound as you yawn; really enjoy the experience.

2. Without losing that relaxed feeling, take a deep breath and pretend that you are blowing the air out through a small drinking straw you are holding in your lips. Let your lips extend in a pucker, and make the smallest hole possible to release the air through that imaginary straw.

3. Now repeat the imaginary straw exercise, this time adding a sound like the wind as you release the air. Some voice teachers call this a buzzing sound. If you are reaching out with your lips and making the sound properly, you will feel the front of your face and your nose vibrate. The more pressure you use to push out the air through your lips, the more vibration you will feel. The sensation indicates that you are placing, or focusing, your voice correctly to get the most resonance or the richest sound.

4. Keeping that forward feeling and the vibrations, slowly repeat the following words: *bring, ling, ming, ning, sing.* Hold onto the *ng* sound and feel the vibrations. Be sure you are getting an *ng* sound, not just an *n* sound.

5. Play with that *ng* sound by pretending that you are a mosquito buzzing around someone's head or a dive bomber flying up and down in the air. Use all parts of your vocal pitch range from the top to the bottom; but keep the *ng* sound forward. Hint: It helps to keep reaching out with your lips forward.

6. Stand comfortably erect with your weight on both feet. Take a deep breath and slowly speak the following lines from "The Creation" with the sound focused forward.

> And God stepped out on space
> And he looked around and said:
> I'm lonely—
> I'll make me a world.
>
> And as far as the eye of God could see
> Darkness covered everything
> Blacker than a hundred midnights
> Down in a cypress swamp.
>
> Then God smiled,
> And the light broke,
> And the darkness rolled up on one side,
> And the light stood shining on the other,
> And God said: That's good!
>
> *James Weldon Johnson* ■

Through the previous exercises you have learned how to breathe correctly, generate sound in the vocal cords, and enrich the sound by placing it forward to take advantage of the cavities in the head. Now you are ready to add the final touches that shape the resonant sound into clear words. This process is called **articulation.** It is the way a speaker makes words distinct and clear.

Some people have lazy mouths: their articulators—the tongue, lips, teeth, soft and hard palates—do not work hard enough, and their words sound muffled or slurred. A good performer must be able to articulate sounds with precision and clarity. Of course, sometimes you may want to portray characters who speak as if their mouths were full of mush; but as a performer, you must be capable of crisp articulation when you need it.

Many people enjoy the challenges of tongue twisters that force precise articulation. Some of these twisters, like "Peter Piper," are so well known they don't need repetition here. Others suggested below may be new or at least less familiar to you.

Activity 8   Articulating Sound

1. Repeat each of these phrases or sentences slowly and clearly. Gradually speed up until you can no longer control the articulation. Then slowly start again and gradually accelerate. Keep working until you can speak the exercises flawlessly at a rapid rate.

   - Toy boat
   - Chrysanthemum, geranium
   - Aluminum, linoleum
   - Red leather, yellow leather
   - Unique New York
   - Rubber baby buggy bumpers
   - Sister Susie's sewing shirts for soldiers.
   - She sells seashells by the seashore.
   - Hither thither watch them slither!
   - Jittery justice just flusters most of us.
   - Are our eyes our own?

2. The following song from Gilbert and Sullivan's operetta *The Pirates of Penzance* makes an excellent exercise to develop crisp articulation. Speak it slowly at first, making sure that you articulate every syllable. Gradually speed up until you can speak the words rapidly without losing the sharp articulation. Be sure to take a deep breath and keep the sound forward.

   > I am the very model of a modern Major-General,
   > I've information vegetable, animal, and mineral,
   > I know the kings of England, and I quote the fights historical,
   > From Marathon to Waterloo, in order categorical;
   > I'm very well acquainted too with matters mathematical,
   > I understand equations, both simple and quadratical,
   > About binomial theorem I'm teeming with a lot of news—
   > With many cheerful facts about the square of the hypotenuse . . . .
   > I'm very good at integral and differential calculus,
   > I know the scientific names of beings animalculous;
   > In short, in matters vegetable, animal, or mineral,
   > I am the very model of a modern Major-General. ∎

3 Analyzing Prose

Come On Down . . .

Imagine that you have been selected to appear on a television quiz show where you could win thousands of dollars. Your category is interpretation. You have breezed through the preliminary rounds where you answered correctly every question posed. Now comes the big challenge: for the grand prize, you are asked to explain the difference between *prose* and *poetry*. Will you win?

The question may seem easy at first, but it's really very tricky. You may answer that poetry rhymes but prose does not; yet the quizmaster may point out that some poetry, such as free verse and blank verse, does not rhyme. You may suggest that poetry features recurrent rhythms while prose does not; but the host may remind you that some poetry does not have a repeated rhythm and that the best prose has a subtle rhythm of its own. You may argue that poetry features heightened language rich in similes, metaphors, and other figures of speech and prose does not; yet the questioner may remind you that the best prose employs these same devices. In frustration you may claim that there is no difference between prose and poetry; and in a sense you would be correct, for the best-written prose is very similar to good poetry. That's why it's sometimes called prose poetry.

To understand the differences between prose and poetry, it may be helpful to think of all written communication as lined up on a continuum. On one end is the best poetry, in which the writer has used the most heightened and richly connotative language an individual can devise to convey the complexity and ambiguity of the experience to be shared. At the other extreme might be a mathematical or scientific formula such as $e = mc^2$. Here the writer wishes to make a totally unambiguous statement stripped of any emotional or connotative meaning that might color the reader's understanding of the concept. Prose would occupy the middle area on the continuum, with writing such as a scientific paper to the left of center, a history textbook near the middle, a biography or imaginative historical account such as Jim Bishop's *The Day Kennedy Was Shot* more to the right, and a fictional prose work such as Emily Brontë's *Wuthering Heights,* which employs highly charged language, very close to the end of the continuum indicated for poetry.

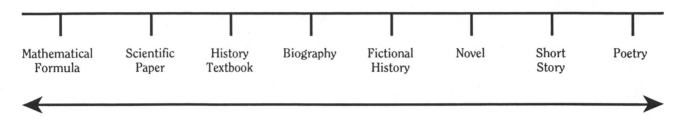

| Mathematical Formula | Scientific Paper | History Textbook | Biography | Fictional History | Novel | Short Story | Poetry |

Works that seek to be free from emotionally charged language, to be unambiguously precise in conveying an abstract intellectual concept

Works that rely more heavily on connotation and heightened language to be ambiguously precise in conveying an emotional experience

As you can see, the categories may overlap: a simple poem like Clement Moore's "The Night Before Christmas," except for its rhyme and recurrent rhythm, uses very much the ordinary, everyday language associated with prose; and a short story like Joseph Conrad's "The Lagoon," with its heightened language rich in imagery and symbolism, uses the devices we associate with poetry.

Prose, a Definition

For the purposes of this textbook, the term **prose** refers to the language of everyday speech. Although it may vary in its richness, it is the language we encounter in most letters, newspaper articles, essays, textbooks, short stories, and novels. Usually it is structured into full sentences combined into paragraphs rather than into individual lines combined into stanzas as in poetry. Although any kind of prose literature may be read aloud effectively—for example, letters, essays, and biographies—this book will focus on the interpretation of **prose fiction,** notably short stories and novels.

Despite their different lengths, these two genres have a number of elements in common. Both involve **actions** or the events that make up the **plot;** both occur in particular places and times, which make up the **settings;** and the events which unfold happen to specific individuals called **characters.** In addition, both short stories and novels are related by specific storytellers called **narrators,** who present each story from a certain perspective or **point of view.** These narrators arrange the events in such a way that they make maximum impacts on their readers/listeners. Although each novel or short story has its unique arrangement, it will usually involve some kind of **conflict** moving from an **inciting action** through a series of minor and major **climaxes** and finally to a resolution, also called the **denouement.**

As an interpreter, you have the responsibility to understand all these elements of the story so well that you make your audience understand and experience the literature more compellingly than they could by reading it themselves. This is an important responsibility; and it will require you to use your intellect, your emotions, and your body to achieve your goal.

Where should you start in your quest to discover the total meaning of a work? As was mentioned in Chapter 1, it is a good idea to read the selection aloud a number of times to let it work on you. Each time you read it and think about it, you will likely discover something new about the characters, the narrator, the events, and even the reasons the author chose to organize the story in the way that he or she did. Your growth in understanding rarely will happen in a straightforward manner. Rather you will experience a series of discoveries or insights—often happening quickly as brainstorms. Gradually you'll be able to put it all together in a richly textured performance.

Plot: What's Going on Here?

For most silent readers of prose fiction, the plot is the main aspect of the story: they read to know the general events or actions that occur. As the interpreter, you must become an expert on the details of the stories and the precise sequence of events. Sometimes even a tiny point may be important to the outcome of a plot, especially in a detective story. While performing, you must be certain to give such a detail sufficient emphasis that the audience remembers it and yet not so much emphasis that you give away the mystery.

In addition, you will find that narrators do not always unfold stories in strict chronological order. Instead they may use digression, flashbacks, or deliberate out-of-sequence episodes to speed up or slow down the action. As the performer/narrator, you must discover why the narrator tells the story in the order chosen and enable your audience to feel the progression or shifts of time as they build to the climax.

Setting: Where Are We?

Many inexperienced readers tend to rush over descriptive passages of the setting to get to the events of the story. As a good interpreter, you can't afford to be so careless. A competent author will not insert words of description unless they are important, and one of your jobs as the interpreter is to discover why the author has taken such pains to make the setting vivid.

The most obvious reason for using extended description is to create a mood. Notice how effectively Edgar Allan Poe creates an atmosphere of gloom as he describes a room in his short story "The Fall of the House of Usher."

> The room in which I found myself was very large and lofty. The windows were long, narrow, and pointed, and at so vast a distance from the black oaken floor as to be altogether inaccessible from within. Feeble gleams of encrimsoned light made their way through the trellised panes, and served to render sufficiently distinct the more prominent objects around; the eye, however, struggled in vain to reach the remoter angles of the chamber, or the recesses of the vaulted and fretted ceiling. Dark draperies hung upon the walls. The general furniture was profuse, comfortless, antique, and tattered. Many books and musical instruments lay scattered about, but failed to give any vitality to the scene. I felt that I breathed an atmosphere of sorrow. An air of stern, deep, and irredeemable gloom hung over and pervaded all.

As an interpreter, you must see that room vividly in your imagination and then take the time to describe it so carefully that your listeners experience the mood of gloom.

Description of setting is also important to create an environment for an action to occur. For example, a vivid description may reveal the time period in which a story is set and thus provide background by which the actions of the characters may be judged. If, for instance, an author were to describe an elaborate formal reception room in a magnificent eighteenth-century English mansion, you might expect the occupants in that setting to behave in the polite and refined manner of aristocratic persons of the time. But if a character in that room sprawled on a delicate settee, put his feet up on a fancy gilt table, and burped loudly, a reader/listener—as well as the other characters in the scene—might be shocked. That same behavior, done in a crudely furnished barroom, might be funny but hardly shocking. Thus the setting can make an important contribution to the way the author wants the reader to view a character's behavior. To be an effective interpreter, you cannot ignore this important function of setting.

Finally, description, because it appeals to the senses, makes the experience described seem real to both the reader and the audience, all of whom respond with their whole bodies. Notice, for example, how Truman Capote uses sensory imagery to immerse the reader/listener in the world he creates in his short story "A Christmas Memory."

> The black stove, stoked with coal and firewood, glows like a lighted pumpkin. Eggbeaters whirl, spoons spin round in bowls of butter and sugar, vanilla sweetens the air, ginger spices it; melting, nose-tingling odors saturate the kitchen, suffuse the house, drift out to the world on puffs of chimney smoke. . . .

Indeed, if an author provides a detailed setting, you must consider that environment an essential element of your performance and present it carefully and imaginatively to stimulate the senses of your audience.

Activity 1   Communicating Images

1. Select the setting created by Poe or the one created by Capote and read it aloud in a way that will capture the imaginations of your listeners. Identify the important words that will appeal to the senses. Don't just *stress* these words; instead *color* them vocally and physically so as to project their sensory qualities.

2. Read your selection to a partner or to a group and have them comment on the effectiveness of sensory images you projected. Did they hear, see, smell, taste, and feel what you conveyed? ■

Characters: Who's Involved?

When you read a story, no doubt you become interested in the characters. As you learned in Chapter 1, you need to know them inside and out so that you can embody them convincingly for your audience. You must be able to suggest their physical characteristics as well as their intellectual, emotional, and psychological traits. Especially you must know *why* they behave as they do. Each line a character says is motivated by a desire to achieve some end, whether that intention is as minor as getting a kind word from a friend or as major as convincing an enemy to spare his or her life. This intention will influence everything the character says and does.

How do you build such detailed understanding? Chapter 1 suggested some of the approaches, and you will discover a more extended explanation of character analysis in Chapter 7. For now, begin by looking at what characters say and do and what other characters say about them. Second, you need to examine *how* the characters speak, for the ways they express themselves reveal a great deal about their intelligence, backgrounds, education, maturity, emotional states, and attitudes. Third, you need to look carefully at characters' relationships with others, for these may reveal conflicts that are extremely important to the power of the story. Through intelligent attention to these matters, you should be able to pick up the information the author has given you. You may then have to imagine additional details that are consistent with what the author has provided in order to round out the characterizations and create complex, believable human beings who will fascinate the audience.

For many years British actor Emlyn Williams performed a one-man show featuring the works of Charles Dickens. Because Dickens' novels are populated by so many characters, many of them eccentric, Williams had to create dozens of characterizations, some for characters who appeared for only a line or two. Yet anyone who saw those remarkable portrayals can testify that Williams made each one clear and distinct. Each had his or her unique posture, degree of tension, facial expression, vocal quality, rate of speech, manner of speaking, and attitude. In addition, Williams made evident the characters' intentions for every line. His work was a model of superb interpretation of prose fiction.

As an inexperienced interpreter, you should not attempt the large cast of characters that Emlyn Williams portrayed; instead begin with a limited number that you can present effectively—perhaps only one—and gradually increase the number as your skills develop. Because it's important to create every character accurately and believably, don't overextend yourself; doing so many result in distorted or unrealistic characterizations. Challenging material, diligent work, and patience are the ingredients for success.

The Narrator: Who's in Charge Here?

The most important character you will present is the narrator of the story, for it is this person who controls the entire performance. One of your first tasks as you prepare your selection is to discover just who that person is and what he or she is like.

Some narrators are relatively easy to know because the author has characterized them so richly. Others are presented more subtly and may be more difficult to comprehend. Usually the narrators of stories written in the first person are easier to characterize than third-person narrators who tell stories in which they do not participate. By what they say about themselves and the way they speak, the first-person narrators reveal a great deal about the kinds of people they are. Look at two examples. The first is the narrator of Tom McAfee's short story "This Is My Living Room."

MY LIVING ROOM

it ain't big but big enough for me and my family—my wife Rosie setting over there reading recipes in the Birmingham *News* and my two girls Ellen Jean and Martha Kay watching the TV. I am setting here holding *Life* magazine in my lap. I get *Life,* the *News,* and *Christian Living*. I read a lots, the newspaper everyday from cover to cover. I don't just look at the pictures in *Life*. I read what's under them and the stories. I consider myself a smart man and I ain't bragging. A man can learn a lots from just watching the TV, if he knows what to watch for and if he listens close. I do. There ain't many that can say that and be truthful. Maybe nobody else in this whole town, which is Pine Springs.

Yonder in the corner, to the other side of the Coca-Cola calendar, is my 12 gauge. When I go in to bed, I take it with me, set it against the wall, loaded, ready to use, so I can use it if I need to. I've used it before and maybe will again. The only one to protect you is yourself and if you don't you're a fool. I got me a pistol and a .22 locked up in the back room. I could use them too.

The reader can tell a great deal about the narrator in these first two paragraphs. First, it's clear that he has a high opinion of himself. He says he's "a smart man" and considers anyone who can't protect himself "a fool." Although he claims not to brag, he does mention that he reads "a lots," including *Christian Living;* and he prides himself for learning so much from close attention to television, an accomplishment he believes makes him superior to others in his town. In addition, he reveals that he lives in Birmingham, Alabama, in a modest home, where he keeps three firearms for protection. From this opening passage, the reader can't tell his exact age, but he's old enough to have two daughters. Later in the story he says that he has been married almost thirty years and that his daughters are fourteen and sixteen.

At the same time, this man reveals a great deal that he may not mean to reveal. His grammar—notice the repeated use of "ain't," and his misuse of words, "setting" for "sitting," for instance—show his lack of education just as his concern for keeping firearms shows his rather obsessive fear for his safety. Further reading makes even more clear his ignorance, bigotry, and cruelty. That such a man would associate himself with Christian values is highly **ironic;** in other words, there is a clear contrast between what appears to be and what really is. The author has indeed provided a vivid and chilling portrait that gives the interpreter a wealth of details for characterization.

Eudora Welty also creates a richly characterized narrator in her short story "Why I Live at the P. O."

> I was getting along fine with Mama, Papa-Daddy and Uncle Rondo until sister Stella-Rondo just separated from her husband and came back home again. Mr. Whitaker! Of course I went with Mr. Whitaker first, when he first appeared here in China Grove, taking "Pose Yourself" photos, and Stella-Rondo broke us up. Told him I was one-sided. Bigger on one side than the other, which is a deliberate, calculated falsehood. I'm the same. Stella-Rondo is exactly twelve months to the day younger than I am and for that reason she's spoiled.
>
> She's always had anything in the world she wanted and then she'd throw it away. Papa-Daddy gave her this gorgeous Add-a-Pearl necklace when she was eight years old and she threw it away playing baseball when she was nine, with only two pearls.
>
> So as soon as she got married and moved away from home the first thing she did was separate! From Mr. Whitaker! The photographer with the popeyes she said she trusted. Came home from one of those towns up in Illinois and to our complete surprise brought this child of two.

Sister, the narrator, speaks from the post office in China Grove, Mississippi, the second-smallest post office in the state. She has moved to this building because of a family quarrel which she claims was caused by her younger sister, Stella-Rondo. As in the previous example, the reader can learn a good deal about the narrator from this brief opening segment.

Although Sister is not stupid, she is no genius. Her speech reveals that she's talkative, even gossipy, as she pours out the family affairs to passersby in the post office. More importantly, most of her gossip concerns her sister Stella-Rondo of whom she's very jealous, perhaps with good reason. As a result she criticizes almost everything Stella-Rondo has done, from throwing away her "gorgeous Add-a-Pearl necklace" at age nine to separating from her husband, a man Sister claims was originally interested in her. Somewhat self-righteous, Sister feels unfairly treated by her mother, grandfather, sister, and Mr. Whitaker. Such a feeling of persecution suggests that she may have a somewhat distorted sense of reality. At the very least, she makes a big fuss about some petty incidents as she attempts to win allies in her listeners. With Sister, Eudora Welty has created a wonderfully comic character who provides an excellent challenge for the interpreter.

Activity 2 Characterizing a First-Person Narrator

1. The following selections are opening passages from works featuring first-person narrators. Study each of the passages and discuss what qualities of the narrator you can pick out to help you build a complex characterization. Some questions you might consider are these:

How old is this narrator?

How well educated is he or she? Pay particular attention to the narrator's grammar and choice of words.

In what part of the world does the narrator live? Note the use of dialect or unusual words for clues.

How intelligent is she or he?

What is the narrator's attitude toward the people or events mentioned?

Why might the narrator be telling the story?

FROM *THE ADVENTURES OF HUCKLEBERRY FINN*
by Mark Twain

You don't know about me without you have read a book by the name of *The Adventures of Tom Sawyer;* but that ain't no matter. That book was made by Mr. Mark Twain, and he told the truth, mainly. There was things which he stretched, but mainly he told the truth. That is nothing. I never seen anybody but lied one time or another, without it was Aunt Polly, or the widow, or maybe Mary. Aunt Polly—Tom's Aunt Polly, she is—and Mary, and the Widow Douglas is all told about in that book, which is mostly a true book, with some stretches, as I said before.

FROM "MY SISTER'S MARRIAGE"
by Cynthia Marshall Rich

When my mother died she left just Olive and me to take care of Father. Yesterday when I burned the package of Olive's letters that left only me. I know that you'll side with my sister in all this because you're only outsiders, and strangers can afford to sympathize with young love, and with whatever sounds daring and romantic, without thinking what it does to all the other people involved. I don't want you to hate my sister—I don't hate her—but I want you to see that we're happier this way, Father and I, and as for Olive, she made her choice.

FROM "ON SATURDAY AFTERNOON"
by Alan Sillitoe

I once saw a bloke try to kill himself. I'll never forget the day because I was sitting in the house one Saturday afternoon, feeling black and fed up because everybody in the family had gone to the pictures, except me who'd for some reason been left out of it. 'Course, I didn't know then that I would see something you can never see in the same way in the pictures, a real bloke stringing himself up. I was only a kid at the time, so you can imagine how much I enjoyed it.

FROM "THE UGLIEST PILGRIM"
by Doris Betts

I sit in the bus station, nipping chocolate peel off a Mounds candy bar with my teeth, then pasting the coconut filling to the roof of my mouth. The lump will dissolve there slowly and seep into me the way dew seeps into flowers.

I like to separate flavors that way. Always I lick the salt off cracker tops before taking the first bite.

Somebody sees me with my suitcase, paper sack, and a ticket in my lap. "You going someplace, Violet?"

Stupid. People in Spruce Pine are dumb and, since I look dumb, say dumb things to me. I turn up my face as if to count those dead flies piled under the light bulb. He walks away—a fat man, could be anybody. I stick out my tongue at his back; the candy oozes down. If I could stop swallowing, it would drip into my lung and I could breathe vanilla.

Whoever it was, he won't glance back. People in Spruce Pine don't like to look at me, full face.

FROM "ONLY THE DEAD KNOW BROOKLYN"
by Thomas Wolfe

Dere's no guy livin' dat knows Brooklyn t'roo an' t'roo, because it'd take a guy a lifetime just to find his way aroun' duh . . . town.

So like I say, I'm waitin' for my train t' come when I see dis big guy standin' deh—dis is duh foist I eveh see of him. Well, he's lookin' wild, y'know, an' I can see dat he's had plenty, but still he's holdin' it; he talks good an' is walkin' straight enough. So den, dis big guy steps up to a little guy dat's standin' deh, an' says, "How d'yuh get t' Eighteent' Avenoo an Sixty-sevent' Street?" he says.

2. Select one of the story openings and present it in an oral performance that shows your ability to capture the character of the first-person narrator. ∎

Finding clues to characterize the narrators of works told in the third person is often more difficult than finding such hints in first-person narratives. The reason is that the narrators are reporting stories that do not involve them and thus the speakers tend to be more objective, to inject less of themselves into the telling. Such a situation makes your task of characterizing the narrator challenging, but it should not deter you from working on a selection told in the third person.

When the narrator is not so clearly defined, you must rely much more on subtle clues to discover the personality of this important character. The vocabulary and grammar the narrator uses, for example, may indicate his or her intelligence, level of education, and attitudes toward the events and characters described; the figures of speech the narrator uses may reveal her or his background, interests, or even profession. Look at the opening of Katherine Mansfield's short story "Miss Brill" to see what hints you can get about the third-person narrator.

Although it was so brilliantly fine—the blue sky powdered with gold and great spots of light like white wine splashed over the Jardins Publiques—Miss Brill was glad that she had decided on her fur. The air was motionless, but when you opened your mouth there was just a faint chill, like a chill from a glass of iced water before you sip, and now and again a leaf came drifting—from nowhere, from the sky. Miss Brill put up her hand and touched her fur. Dear little thing! It was nice to feel it again. She had taken it out of its box that afternoon, shaken out the moth powder, given it a good brush, and rubbed the life back into the dim little eyes. "What has been happening to me?" said the sad little eyes. Oh, how sweet it was to see them snap at her again from the red eiderdown! . . . But the nose, which was of some black composition, wasn't at all firm. It must have had a knock, somehow. Never mind—a little dab of black sealing-wax when the time came—when it was absolutely necessary. . . . Little rogue! Yes, she really felt like that about it. Little rogue biting its tail just by her left ear. She could have taken it off and laid it on her lap and stroked it. She felt a tingling in her hands and arms, but that came from walking, she supposed. And when she breathed, something light and sad—no, not sad, exactly—something gentle seemed to move in her bosom.

Perhaps the first thing you noticed was the narrator's sensitivity to the weather, expressed in vivid figures of speech. The narrator is aware of the fine scene, the blue sky, the quality of the light, the still air, the faint chill. Obviously this individual has a lively enjoyment of the setting.

The narrator's enjoyment of the scene combines with a sensitive empathy with Miss Brill herself. The narrator knows Miss Brill very well and understands that Miss Brill regards her fur piece as if it were a pet with a personality and feelings. It would be easy for the narrator to make fun of this lonely little spinster who treats an article of clothing in such a manner, but the narrator does not find Miss Brill silly. Rather this individual shares Miss Brill's attitude and understands her affection. You will notice that the narrator even understands such subtle qualities about Miss Brill as her unwillingness to acknowledge sadness. The narrator, in fact, seems so like the character that a performer could probably characterize her as a woman almost identical to Miss Brill, an elderly and somewhat old-fashioned person whose life seems very lonely.

Because Katherine Mansfield is a masterful writer of great sensitivity and subtlety, the narrator's traits may become apparent to you only after several careful readings of the story. As the interpreter, you must find them and show them through your performance so that your audience, hearing the story only once, can know the narrator and share the experience. Whenever you encounter a third-person storyteller, your task will be the same: to dig into the story and pull out all the clues that will help you establish a complete, fleshed-out characterization for that narrator.

Point of View: Do You See What I See?

Having explored the personalities of the characters and the narrator, you need to consider one other important aspect of prose fiction, the point of view from which the story is told.

What is the **point of view**? It is the place from which the narrator relates the story. It is determined by the narrator's physical *location* in relation to the events of the story, the *time* that has elapsed between the events and the narrator's telling of them, and the narrator's *role* in the story. Those three considerations will define the way the narrator tells the story and consequently the way the story affects the readers.

Imagine that you and your best friend get into a heated argument in a hall at school. The disagreement and anger grow until the altercation explodes into a knock-down-drag-out fight. Other students who have been watching the whole affair eventually pull you, panting and struggling, from each other. The principal arrives and asks what happened. The story of the fight may be told from any number of perspectives.

You could tell the story on the spot. You were right there; in fact, you were a major participant in the event. In terms of time you are still breathless from the emotional experience. You certainly have a biased viewpoint, however, because you want to prove that you were in the right.

Your best friend could also tell his or her side of the story. Your friend's point of view would be similar to yours in terms of location, time, and role; and yet her or his version might be very different from yours because of the different bias and intention.

The story might also be told by one of the students who pulled you apart. This individual would be less emotionally involved than you but was nonetheless a minor participant in the situation, very closely observing it and perhaps taking the side of you or your best friend.

Or the story might be told by another student who doesn't know you and who watched the events from a spot forty feet away. That person, uninvolved in the action and more curious than emotionally affected, certainly could not have observed all the details of the encounter.

Finally, the story might be retold by someone who was not in the building but who had heard about the incident from someone else. Of course, that person's account of the story would be different from all others depending on the particular version he or she had heard. No doubt this person would hear very different treatments if told by you, your best friend, the student who pulled you apart, the student down the hall, or your mother!

The situation becomes more complex when the element of time enters the picture. Your telling of the story immediately after the fight would be somewhat different from the version you would tell the next day, after you had had time to calm down, or the next week, after you and your best friend had patched up your differences. And of course the version you might tell your grandchildren fifty years later would be *very* different. Usually the more distant you get from an event, the less emotional you are about it and the more objective you become. Often, however, you will forget details, and sometimes your mind will color events or create elements that did not exist. Later in life you may even find humor in your behavior as you reexamine it.

Activity 3   Playing with Point of View

The following activity is designed for a small group or for an entire class. Depending on the number of students involved, there may need to be a rotation with some participants taking more than one role.

1. Imagine that the fight discussed above has just occurred, and for interest imagine that it resulted from a romantic triangle. Briefly relate the story as you would present it given your role, your location during the fight, your listener, and the time that has elapsed since the fight occurred.

    You will notice that the last five roles involve people who did not see the fight but only heard about it from others, who may have been partial to one of the fighters or may have not known either one. Their feelings for the two most directly involved and their feelings about fighting in general will also influence the way they report the story.

Role	Location During Fight	Listener	Time Elapsed
Fighter A	Spot where fight occurred	Principal	15 seconds later
Fighter A	Spot where fight occurred	Your mother	Later that evening
Fighter A	Spot where fight occurred	Your cousin	A week later
Fighter A	Spot where fight occurred	Your grandchild	50 years later
Fighter B	Spot where fight occurred	Principal	15 seconds later
Fighter B	Spot where fight occurred	Your father	Later that evening
Fighter B	Spot where fight occurred	A psychologist	2 days later
Fighter B	Spot where fight occurred	Your biographer	50 years later

(Continued)

Role	Location During Fight	Listener	Time Elapsed
Bystander	5 feet from fight	Principal	10 minutes later
Bystander	5 feet from fight	Good friend	The next morning
Bystander	5 feet from fight	College friend	7 years later
Student in hall	40 feet from fight	Teacher	30 seconds later
Student in hall	40 feet from fight	Good friend	Later that evening
Gossip	In public library	Fellow gossip	The next morning
A's Mother	In kitchen at home	Neighbor	The next afternoon
B's Mother	At work at a law firm	Lawyer	The next morning
Custodian	In custodian's closet	Fellow custodian	1 hour later
Principal	In his office	Wife	Later that evening

2. Discuss differences that appeared in the stories as told by each of the narrators. How did a person's proximity to the event and the elapsed time influence the way he or she told the story? How did each narrator's intention determine the way she or he told the story?

3. How can you apply what you learned from this activity to the works of prose fiction you prepare for performance? ■

Identifying Points of View

As you know, it is customary to refer to the narrators of prose fiction as first-person narrators or as third-person narrators. Second-person narrators are extremely rare: you may never encounter one in your reading.

The first-person narrative is easy to spot as the narrator constantly refers to himself or herself as *I*. Usually the person seems to be speaking directly to the readers/listeners about an event in which he or she is a main character; sometimes the narrator relates a story in which she or he was involved but was not a central character; and sometimes the narrator relates incidents that he or she observed or was told about without being an actual participant. You may be familiar with these points of view if you have read two fictional works popular with young readers.

The first kind of narration is illustrated by Huckleberry Finn, the teenaged narrator of Mark Twain's *The Adventures of Huckleberry Finn*. Huck tells his personal story shortly after the main event occurs. The second kind of first-person narration is illustrated by Harper Lee's novel *To Kill a Mockingbird*. This novel's narrator is Jean Louise Finch, nicknamed "Scout"; but she is not the main character. She tells the story of her father, Atticus Finch, a lawyer living in Alabama during the Great Depression. Although she has been involved in the events that she narrates, she is not the central figure. Unlike Huck, Scout is an adult when she tells the story; but the events she relates occurred years earlier when she was a child. Mark Twain's short story "The Celebrated Jumping Frog of Calaveras County" illustrates the uninvolved narrator. This narrator mainly retells a story he heard from a talkative old man named Simon Wheeler. While the narrator is not totally uninvolved because a question he asks Wheeler motivates the old man to tell the tale, this unnamed narrator is not a participant in the story Wheeler relates. He merely reports what he saw and heard from Wheeler.

Third-person narrators tell other people's stories. They may or may not have observed the events they relate, but they have not participated in them. Sometimes they put together stories after observing some of the events and hearing about others. They may be *objective narrators* who report a story as unemotionally as a camera would record it; they may be *omniscient narrators,* all-knowing personalities who have access to the thoughts and feelings existing in the minds of all the characters; or they may be *narrators of limited omniscience,* knowing the thoughts and feelings of only one character. Usually, however, they have some empathy for the main character whose story they relate, and they tell that person's story because it has had some impact on them and because they think it has some significance.

As an interpreter you must be aware of narrators' feelings for the characters they present and of their attitudes toward the events of the story. Then you must convey these feelings and attitudes through your performance to your audience.

One final caution: As you have seen in the brief excerpt from "This is My Living Room," narrators—especially first-person narrators—often have distorted views of themselves, the people who oppose them, and the events they relate. Such storytellers are called **unreliable narrators,** and they need to be treated carefully. Thus as you analyze and perform literature, be aware that any narrator is biased to some degree and that this bias influences his or her intention in telling the story. Some narrators have such intense biases that their reality is distorted. Do your best to discover such biases and distortions so that you are not misled in your interpretive choices. At the same time, you must convey these characters so vividly to your audience that your listeners are able to perceive and question what such narrators tell them. Audiences get a particular pleasure from catching this "double vision" between what the unreliable narrator and the characters tell them and what the real situation is. Be certain your performance enables your listeners to enjoy this special irony.

Activity 4   Extending Your Learning

1. Select three short stories from another literature collection, read the beginning paragraph or paragraphs of each, and determine the point of view of the narrator. Consider the narrator's physical location, the elapsed time, his or her role in the event, and the intention for telling the story. With a partner, go over the opening paragraphs each has chosen and see if you agree.

2. In Activity 3 you dealt with the following narrator roles: Fighter A, Fighter B, Bystander, Student in hall, Gossip, A's Mother, B's Father, Custodian, Principal. Discuss the degree of reliability or unreliability these storytellers might have as they tell about the fight. ■

4 Prose, from Printed Page to Performance

Once Upon a Time . . .

Do you remember learning to read aloud in elementary school? Sometimes the process was painful—both for reader and for listeners! Becoming an adequate oral reader is not easy; but with effort, most students improve. Now you want to be more than adequate. You want to be dynamic.

To move in that direction, you must put your knowledge about the fundamental aspects of prose fiction to practical use. Now you are ready to move through a step-by-step analysis of a short story to prepare it for performance. The work is Edgar Allan Poe's "The Cask of Amontillado," a tale that has remained popular for a century and a half.

A Story to Study

First, read the following selection from Poe's tale aloud to get a general sense of the plot, the organization, and the characters, including the narrator.

THE CASK OF AMONTILLADO

The thousand injuries of Fortunato I had borne as I best could; but when he ventured upon insult, I vowed revenge. You, who so well know the nature of my soul, will not suppose, however, that I gave utterance to a threat. *At length* I would be avenged; this was a point definitively settled—but the very definitiveness with which it was resolved, precluded the idea of risk. I must not only punish, but punish with impunity. A wrong is unredressed when retribution overtakes its redresser. It is equally unredressed when the avenger fails to make himself felt as such to him who has done the wrong.

It must be understood, that neither by word nor deed had I given Fortunato cause to doubt my good-will. I continued, as was my wont, to smile in his face, and he did not perceive that my smile *now* was at the thought of his immolation.

He had a weak point—this Fortunato—although in other regards he was a man to be respected and even feared. He prided himself on his connoisseurship of wine.

Few Italians have the true virtuoso spirit. For the most part their enthusiasm is adopted to suit the time and opportunity—to practice imposture upon the British and Austrian millionaires. In painting and gemmary Fortunato, like his countrymen, was a quack—but in the matter of old wines he was sincere. In this respect I did not differ from him materially. I was skillful in the Italian vintages myself, and bought largely whatever I could.

It was about dusk, one evening during the supreme madness of the carnival season, that I encountered my friend. He accosted me with excessive warmth, for he had been drinking much. The man wore motley. He had on a tight fitting parti-striped dress, and his head was surmounted by the conical cap and bells. I was so pleased to see him, that I thought I should never have done wringing his hand.

I said to him: "My dear Fortunato, you are luckily met. How remarkably well you are looking today! But I have received a pipe of what passes for Amontillado, and I have my doubts."

"How?" said he. "Amontillado? A pipe? Impossible! And in the middle of the carnival!"

"I have my doubts," I replied; "and I was silly enough to pay the full Amontillado price without consulting you in the matter. You were not to be found, and I was fearful of losing a bargain."

"Amontillado!"

"I have my doubts."

"Amontillado!"

"And I must satisfy them."

"Amontillado!"

"As you are engaged, I am on my way to Luchesi. If anyone has a critical turn, it is he. He will tell me—"

"Luchesi cannot tell Amontillado from Sherry."

"And yet some fools will have it that his taste is a match for your own."

"Come, let us go."

"Whither?"

"To your vaults."

"My friend, no; I will not impose upon your good nature. I perceive you have an engagement. Luchesi—"

"I have no engagement; come."

"My friend, no. It is not the engagement, but the severe cold with which I perceive you are afflicted. The vaults are insufferably damp. They are encrusted with nitre."

"Let us go, nevertheless. The cold is merely nothing. Amontillado! You have been imposed upon. And as for Luchesi, he cannot distinguish Sherry from Amontillado."

Thus speaking, Fortunato possessed himself of my arm. Putting on a mask of black silk, and drawing a *roquelaire* closely about my person, I suffered him to hurry me to my palazzo.

There were no attendants at home; they had absconded to make merry in honor of the time. I had told them that I should not return until the morning, and had given them explicit orders not to stir from the house. These orders were sufficient, I well knew, to insure their immediate disappearance, one and all, as soon as my back was turned.

I took from their sconces two flambeaux, and giving one to Fortunato, bowed him through several suites of rooms to an archway that led into the vaults. I passed down a long winding staircase, requesting him to be cautious as he followed. We came at length to the foot of the descent, and stood together on the damp ground of the catacombs of the Montresors.

The gait of my friend was unsteady, and the bells upon his cap jingled as he strode.

"The pipe?" said he.

"It is farther on," said I; "but observe the white web-work which gleams from these cavern walls."

He turned toward me, and looked into my eyes with two filmy orbs that distilled the rheum of intoxication.

"Nitre?" he asked, at length.

"Nitre," I replied. "How long have you had that cough?"

"Ugh! ugh! ugh!—ugh! ugh! ugh!—ugh! ugh! ugh!—ugh! ugh! ugh!—ugh! ugh! ugh!"

My poor friend found it impossible to reply for many minutes.

"It is nothing," he said, at last.

"Come," I said, with decision, "we will go back; your health is precious. You are rich, respected, admired, beloved; you are happy, as once I was. You are a man to be missed. For me it is no matter. We will go back; you will be ill, and I cannot be responsible. Besides, there is Luchesi—"

"Enough," he said; "the cough is a mere nothing; it will not kill me. I shall not die of a cough."

"True—true," I replied; "and, indeed, I had no intention of alarming you unnecessarily; but you should use all proper caution. A draught of this Medoc will defend us from the damps."

Here I knocked off the neck of a bottle which I drew from a long row of its fellows that lay upon the mould.

"Drink," I said, presenting him the wine.

He raised it to his lips with a leer. He paused and nodded to me familiarly, while his bells jingled.

"I drink," he said, "to the buried that repose around us."

"And I to your long life."

He again took my arm, and we proceeded.

"These vaults," he said, "are extensive."

"The Montresors," I replied, "were a great and numerous family."

"I forget your arms."

"A huge human foot d'or, in a field azure; the foot crushes a serpent rampant whose fangs are imbedded in the heel."

"And the motto?"

"*Nemo me impune lacessit.*"

"Good!" he said.

The wine sparkled in his eyes and the bells jingled. My own fancy grew warm with the Medoc. We had passed through the walls of piled bones, with casks and puncheons intermingling into the inmost recesses of the catacombs. I paused again, and this time I made bold to seize Fortunato by an arm above the elbow.

"The nitre!" I said; "see, it increases. It hangs like moss upon the vaults. We are below the river's bed. The drops of moisture trickle among the bones. Come, we will go back ere it is too late. Your cough—"

"It is nothing," he said; "let us go on. But first, another draught of the Medoc."

I broke and reached him a flagon of De Grave. He emptied it at a breath. His eyes flashed with a fierce light. He laughed and threw the bottle upward with a gesticulation I did not understand.

I looked at him in surprise. He repeated the movement—a grotesque one.

"You do not comprehend?" he said.

"Not I," I replied.

"Then you are not of the brotherhood."

"How?"

"You are not of the masons."

"Yes, yes," I said; "yes, yes."

"You! Impossible! A mason?"

"A mason," I replied.

"A sign," he said.

"It is this," I answered, producing a trowel from beneath the folds of my *roquelaire.*

"You jest," he exclaimed, recoiling a few paces. "But let us proceed to the Amontillado."

"Be it so," I said, replacing the tool beneath the cloak, and again offering him my arm. He leaned upon it heavily. We continued our route in search of the Amontillado. We passed through a range of low arches, descended, passed on, and descending again, arrived at a deep crypt, in which the foulness of the air caused our flambeaux rather to glow than flame.

At the most remote end of the crypt there appeared another less spacious. Its walls had been lined with human remains, piled to the vault overhead, in the fashion of the great catacombs of Paris. Three sides of this interior crypt were still ornamented in this manner. From the fourth the bones had been thrown down, and lay promiscuously upon the earth, forming at one point a mound of some size. Within the wall thus exposed by the displacing of the bones, we perceived a still interior recess, in depth about four feet, in width three, in height six or seven. It seemed to have been constructed for no especial use within itself, but formed merely the interval between two of the colossal supports of the roof of the catacombs, and was backed by one of their circumscribing walls of solid granite.

It was in vain that Fortunato, uplifting his dull torch, endeavored to pry into the depth of the recess. Its termination the feeble light did not enable us to see.

"Proceed," I said; "herein is the Amontillado. As for Luchesi—"

"He is an ignoramus," interrupted my friend, as he stepped unsteadily forward, while I followed immediately at his heels. In an instant he had reached the extremity of the niche, and finding his progress arrested by the rock, stood stupidly bewildered. A moment more and I had fettered him to the granite. In its surface were two iron staples, distant from each other about two feet, horizontally. From one of these depended a short chain, from the other a padlock. Throwing the links about his waist, it was but the work of a few seconds to secure it. He was too much astounded to resist. Withdrawing they key I stepped back from the recess.

"Pass your hands," I said, "over the wall; you cannot help feeling the nitre. Indeed it is *very* damp. Once more let me *implore* you to return. No? Then I must positively leave you. But I must first render you all the little attentions in my power."

"The Amontillado!" ejaculated my friend, not yet recovered from his astonishment.

"True," I replied, "the Amontillado."

As I said these words I busied myself among the pile of bones of which I have before spoken. Throwing them aside, I soon uncovered a quantity of building stone and mortar. With these materials and with the aid of my trowel, I began vigorously to wall up the entrance of the niche.

I had scarcely laid the first tier of the masonry when I discovered that the intoxication of Fortunato had in a great measure worn off. The earliest indication I had of this was a low moaning cry from the depth of the recess. It was *not* the cry of a drunken man. There was then a long and obstinate silence. I laid the second tier, and the third, and the fourth; and then I heard the furious vibrations of the chain. The noise lasted for several minutes, during which, that I might harken to it with the more satisfaction, I ceased my labors and sat down upon the bones. When at last the clanking subsided, I resumed the trowel, and finished without interruption the fifth, the sixth, and the seventh tier. The wall was now nearly upon a level with my breast. I again paused, and holding the flambeau over the mason-work, threw a few feeble rays upon the figure within.

A succession of loud and shrill screams, bursting suddenly from the throat of the chained form, seemed to thrust me violently back. For a brief moment I hesitated— I trembled. Unsheathing my rapier, I began to grope with it about the recess; but the thought of an instant reassured me. I placed my hand upon the solid fabric of the catacombs, and felt satisfied. I reapproached the wall. I replied to the yells of him who clamored. I reechoed—I aided—I surpassed them in volume and in strength. I did this, and the clamorer grew still.

It was now midnight, and my task was drawing to a close. I had completed the eighth, the ninth, and the tenth tier. I had finished a portion of the last and the eleventh; there remained but a single stone to be fitted and plastered in. I struggled with its weight; I placed it partially in its destined position. But now there came from out the niche a low laugh that erected the hairs upon my head. It was succeeded by a sad voice, which I had difficulty in recognizing as that of the noble Fortunato. The voice said—

"Ha! ha! ha!—he! he! he!—a very good joke indeed—an excellent jest. We will have many a rich laugh about it at the palazzo—he! he! he!—over our wine—he! he! he!"

"The Amontillado!" I said.

"He! he! he!—he! he! he!—yes, the Amontillado. But is it not getting late? Will not they be awaiting us at the palazzo, the Lady Fortunato and the rest? Let us be gone?"

"Yes," I said, "let us be gone."

"For the love of God, Montresor!"

"Yes," I said, "for the love of God!"

But to these words I harkened in vain for a reply. I grew impatient. I called aloud:

"Fortunato!"

No answer. I called again.

"Fortunato!"

No answer still. I thrust a torch through the remaining aperture and let it fall within. There came forth in return only a jingling of bells. My heart grew sick—on account of the dampness of the catacombs. I hastened to make an end of my labor. I forced the last stone into its position; I plastered it up. Against the new masonry I re-erected the old rampart of bones. For the half of a century no mortal has disturbed them. *In pace requiescat!*

Activity 1   Understanding Every Word

1. In reading the selection from "The Cask of Amontillado," you no doubt encountered some words that were unfamiliar to you. Because misunderstanding even a single word can mean a misinterpretation, it is important to keep track of words with which you have difficulty and use a dictionary, as needed, noting pronunciations and definitions on a list.

    Following is a list of some words from the selection that may be unfamiliar and may appear on your list.

Amontillado	immolation	nitre	flambeaux	promiscuously
precluded	connoisseurship	roquelaire	catacombs	fettered
impunity	virtuoso	palazzo	draught	termination
redress	gemmary	abscond	puncheons	ignoramus
retribution	motley	sconces	crypt	implore

2. Speak each word on your list aloud several times until you can consistently and easily pronounce the word correctly.

3. Two Latin expressions were used in the story: *"Nemo me impune lacessit"* and *"In pace requiescat."* Learn what they mean and how they should be pronounced. You might check the foreign words and phrases section of an English dictionary, or consult a Latin dictionary in the library. ■

Knowing the Narrator

The next task is to discover all you can about the narrator. From reading "The Cask of Amontillado" you have no doubt discovered that he is a wealthy aristocrat of the once-great Montresor family, that he occupies the ancient family palace with its underground vaults serving as burial chambers for his ancestors, that he cannot bear to be insulted, and that he is obsessed with gaining secret and absolute revenge. These are qualities that most readers will grasp upon first reading or hearing the story.

As a future performer of this story, you must probe deeper than the average reader. You must catch the more subtle qualities of Montresor. For example, how old is he? The answer may surprise you. Notice in the last sentence that he explains that he entombed Fortunato a half-century earlier. Since he is an adult at the time of the murder, he must now be an elderly man, in his seventies at the very least. Certainly that fact is important to your characterization of him.

Second, if you read carefully you will note that Montresor is unusually sensitive to behavior that he believes slights him. Notice that in the first line he speaks of the "thousand injuries" which Fortunato has done to him, all of which were less serious than insults. Could he be exaggerating or even imagining the slights? When Fortunato appears later he shows no evidence of such lack of respect or unkindness; indeed, he seems very eager to be helpful to Montresor in judging the wine and goes into the damp vault despite a bad cough and a previous appointment. Thus Montresor, from the beginning, seems intensely eccentric in his judgment. This quality must be evident—but not overly obvious—to your audience from the first sentence Montresor speaks.

Also notice that Montresor delights in his own cleverness in arranging the murder. Not only is his plan cruel, but he takes special pleasure in making jokes about Fortunato's approaching death. When Fortunato says that he won't die of a cough, Montresor replies, "True—true"; and when Fortunato asks if Montresor is a mason, the would-be murderer says he is and produces a trowel he will later use to entomb Fortunato to punctuate his cruel pun. He even drinks an ironic toast to Fortunato's long life.

Finally, to round out your understanding of Montresor's character, you need to ask what has driven the then-young man to such a state of mental illness. He gives readers only a few clues. He says that Fortunato is happy as once Montresor himself was. Apparently he has for some reason become unhappy. A further clue is more subtle. Montresor uses the past tense when he says the Montresors "were a great and numerous family." Apparently the family is no longer what it was in power and numbers. In fact, Montresor seems to be the only member still alive as he and his attendants or servants appear to be the only ones living in the palace. What misfortunes have reduced Montresor to this unhappy state where he is overly sensitive to insults and distrustful of everyone, including his own servants? You as the interpreter can imaginatively decide that answer because there is no specific answer in the text. Perhaps his family was killed by the plague; perhaps they had a shipping business destroyed by a storm that sank all their ships; perhaps someone he trusted cheated him out of his fortune. You as the interpreter can create the most extensive background to make Montresor a character of depth and realism—as long as what you invent in no way contradicts what Poe has provided you in the text.

Knowing what you do about Montresor, you are prepared to embody him or physically to create his character. Here you have a particularly challenging assignment. You know that Montresor is old, and yet he tells of events that happened when he was young. In a sense, then, you will need to present the characterizations of the narrator and main character, one young and one old. How is that possible?

Two possibilities exist. First, you may have the old Montresor tell the entire story. He could make adjustments in his voice and body to suggest the younger Montresor and Fortunato when he reports what they said. The choice would give the old Montresor the central focus of the story and make it seem more a psychological character study than a tale of ghastly revenge.

A second possibility is to speak only the narrative lines as the old Montresor and speak the **direct discourse,*** the exact words of Fortunato and the young Montresor, as the men would speak at their respective ages. Thus their direct conversations would appear more vivid—like movie flashbacks—and the central focus of the story would fall on the plot rather than the character of the narrator.

You must decide which of these two possibilities you think is the more appropriate choice. No matter which choice you make, you must be able to embody the old Montresor and at least suggest the younger one.

Because Montresor tells his story with such sophisticated vocabulary and such vivid verbs, he appears to be younger than his years. Thus it would not be appropriate to make him senile. Rather he appears to be a vigorous man. Though his shoulders may be slightly rounded and his weight centered on the heels of his feet, you must remember that this man is a proud aristocrat. He would probably carry his head high and speak with authority, control, and precise articulation. He might even look down his nose at those he feels are inferior to him. You know from his actions that he is a sly man, not at all straightforward with Fortunato. You might be able to convey that craftiness through your eyes. If you turn your head slightly to the side but turn your eyes to the opposite side, you may convey such a quality. Try looking at something out of the corners of your eyes this way and see if you can capture that impression of duplicity. Perhaps a somewhat forced smile would complete that sense of his insincerity. Finally, let his gestures be easy and graceful to suggest his aristocratic refinement.

Activity 2   Creating a Secondary Character

1. Now that you have characterized the narrator, you need to go through a similar process to characterize Fortunato. Because he's a secondary character, the author has not provided as much detail about him. Begin by exploring the answers to the questions that follow. Write out your answers so that you can consult them during your preparation phase.

---

* The opposite of direct discourse is **indirect discourse,** reported or paraphrased dialogue.

- How old is Fortunato? How do you know?
- What is Fortunato's social rank and position?
- How good is his health? How physically strong is he? Is he a match for Montresor?
- Does he have a drinking problem? What evidence do you have?
- Does he like Montresor? Does he trust him? How do you know?
- Do you believe that he has repeatedly slighted and then insulted Montresor? Give as least one reason for your answer.
- What is the importance of his being a mason?
- How does he relate to Montresor? What does he do to show his feelings?
- Does he have qualities that make you like him? If so, what are they?

2. Now translate physical qualities that will enable your audience to "see" Fortunato in your body. Again, write out your decisions so that you can refer to them as you rehearse.
   - How will Fortunato stand? Will he be erect or stooped?
   - Will he have great bodily tension, or will he be relaxed and loose?
   - What will you do with your eyes to show that Fortunato is having trouble seeing in the dimly lighted passageway?
   - What will his voice be like? Will it be full or thin in quality?
   - Will he have a faster or slower rate of speaking than Montresor?
   - How will his drinking affect the way he moves and speaks?
   - How will he look at Montresor and speak to him to show his feelings for the man? ■

Having considered the physical embodiment of the character, you need to turn your attention to the narrator's reasons for telling this story. Montresor apparently is addressing someone he knows well, for he says, "You, who so well know the nature of my soul . . ." Why would this old man confess a murder he has concealed for fifty years? Poe doesn't give a hint of his reason; as a result you must make a logical choice. Remember that the *reason* for telling the story influences the *way* the narrator tells it.

Activity 3 Conveying Intentions

1. Examine each of the following possibilities for telling the story of "The Cask of Amontillado" and devise at least one other of your own. Consider the plausibility of each and the effect of each in the way the narrator would unfold the tale.
   - He is telling the story *to confess* to a priest a crime that has troubled his conscience for fifty years.
   - He is telling the story *to impress* a fellow aristocrat that he has succeeded in achieving the perfect crime.
   - He is telling the story *to dissuade* his grandson from remodeling the catacombs and thus exposing Fortunato's body.
   - He is telling the story *to justify* to his wife, the former Lady Fortunato, his murder of her first husband.
   - He is telling the story *to threaten* an associate about what fate could await him if he double-crosses Montresor.

2. In a group, discuss what each of you decided independently. Then have each group member justify which approach she or he would take.

3. Read aloud a passage from the story to convey the intention you have chosen. Discuss with the group whether you made the intention clear. ∎

Once you have chosen a reason for the narrator's telling the story, be certain to speak his words to reflect that choice. If that choice for some reason doesn't seem to be convincing, don't be afraid to experiment with another option. Also be sure that your choice does not keep you from expressing the sarcasm Montresor uses such as when he refers to Fortunato as "my good friend" after describing his coughing fit.

Having decided the old Montresor's reason for speaking, you next need to consider the young Montresor's intentions as he entices Fortunato into the vaults. You know that Montresor's ultimate goal is to get revenge for an insult by Fortunato. Now go through the story line-by-line to trace Montresor's method of persuading Fortunato to accompany him. Notice how he takes advantage of Fortunato's pride as a wine expert and his jealousy of Luchesi's skills. Also notice how, after arousing Fortunato's determination to judge the Amontillado, he pretends to be so concerned about Fortunato's health that he advises him not to continue. Capture the conflict between Fortunato's determination to go into the vaults and Montresor's false attempts to dissuade him. Let every line the characters speak be motivated by an attempt to achieve some goal or to influence the other person to some degree. The story will have more tension if you can suggest that, despite his assurances, Fortunato has increasing fear about continuing into the crypt. Perhaps that's why he keeps reinforcing himself with wine. Let every line have a purpose in revealing the character's intentions and building the scene to a climax.

Staging the Setting

As indicated in the previous chapter, the setting in prose fiction demands careful attention. This story makes particularly good use of setting, especially near the end. As Montresor and Fortunato descend into the crypt, you must take time to create the mood for murder by making your audience imagine and feel the environment Montresor creates. He carefully describes the darkness, broken by the flaming torches; the cold dampness; the trickling water; the feel of the nitre; the foul-smelling air; the ghastly piles of human bones. At the end Montresor recalls hideous sounds: Fortunato's moans, screams, and laughter; his clanking chains and pitiful jingling bells; Montresor's own yells. Let all these sound images play in your audience's minds like a sound track of a movie.

Setting also includes the time period of the story. This narrative seems set in the distant past, perhaps the 1500s, when aristocrats like Montresor still lived in cavernous palaces and wielded great power. Also, Poe's selection of carnival time with the elaborate costumes and masks makes the story take on a nightmarish quality. Especially consider the horror of Fortunato, dressed as a medieval court jester, moving through the bone-littered crypt as he is led to his cruel execution. Make your audience shudder at that horrible incongruity.

Dealing with Dialogue

Earlier you saw the two possibilities for handling the story's dialogue: letting the old Montresor tell the entire story in his own persona or letting the young Montresor and Fortunato emerge as fully embodied characters in their own right. If you choose the second option—and you should at least explore it—how will you bring these characters to life in your performance?

The usual approach is to select a spot slightly above the heads of your audience and just behind them and visualize the listening character there. This spot is called the speaking character's **focal point** or point of focus. It is here the speaker directs his or her voice, eyes, and energy. When you shift to the other character, you select another point, just to the left or right of the original one, for the other character to direct her or his focus. As you bodily shift from one character to another, you also shift your focal point; the more characters you portray, the more focal points you will have.

As you perform this altering dialogue, you will need to deal with another problem: what should you do with the dialogue tags, those statements such as "she asked at length" and "he exclaimed, recoiling a few paces" that precede or follow the speaker's exact words? The answer is that you may eliminate them if their only purpose is to identify the speakers and the manner in which they say those words. By the way you speak the lines, you can make clear which character is speaking and the attitude he or she is expressing. Thus one passage from "The Cask of Amontillado" would really be spoken this way:

> "You do not comprehend?"
> "Not I."
> "Then you are not of the brotherhood."
> "How?"
> "You are not of the masons."
> "Yes, yes, yes, yes."
> "You? Impossible! A mason?"

Through quick shifts of body, voice, and focal point, you could make this passage vivid for your audience and give it a sense of dramatic tension that might be lessened if you had to interrupt the flow by speaking the tags.

Tasteful Trimming

Often you will need to prepare a performance to fit a required time limit, such as that imposed by a class assignment or a contest. Then you must either cut out some of the text to condense it or perform just a segment of the work. Both choices need careful consideration.

A well-written work of literature has been so carefully constructed by its author that it can rarely be cut without damage. Any time words are eliminated, the rhythms of the work are disturbed, and characters' motivations often seem altered. Even the removal of the dialogue tags discussed earlier may cause problems. Thus it is better not to do internal cutting if you can avoid it. Usually it is better to perform an uncut excerpt of a long work. By doing such an excerpt, you can maintain the unity of the work without distortion. If, for example, you need to eliminate an extensive part of the story, consider beginning your reading later into the story and using your introduction to give your audience the background they need to understand the excerpt. In Poe's story you might start at the paragraph beginning "The wine sparkled in his eyes and the bells jingled" and perform only the second half of the narrative. In a longer work such as a novel, you may choose to perform only a short episode, such as one of those presented at the end of this chapter. At any rate, the excerpt you select should have a sense of completeness in itself, and it should move to some sort of climax, even if subtle.

If you *must* do some internal cutting, what can you remove with the least harm to a work? First, it is sometimes possible to take out a minor character. Doing so may not only shorten the selection but simplify your preparation by reducing the number of characters you portray. Another possibility is to eliminate extended passages of description. Sometimes you can create the necessary mood with less description than the author provides. Likewise, if you are working with a lengthy short story or a novel, you may cut a digression or a passage that is a preparation for an incident that comes much later in the work and has no direct bearing on the section you perform. Finally, you may remove a portion that provides mainly a special effect, such as the discussion of Montresor's coat of arms, which underscores the theme of revenge but is not absolutely essential. Notice, however, that without this brief passage the narrative flow is not quite as smooth as it is with the passage intact. Because internal cutting almost always causes some such difficulty, the interpreter is wise to limit it as much as possible.

Miscellaneous Matters

Every story presents its particular challenges for the interpreter. "The Cask of Amontillado" has two that you need to meet. First, how should you handle Fortunato's coughing? If you can perform it believably, you should probably perform the spasm in the character of Fortunato. If you cannot do a convincing cough, you might eliminate that spasm and let Fortunato speak his next line "It is nothing" with great difficulty, indicating his struggle to suppress his cough. You certainly would not say, "Ugh! ugh! ugh!" as though each were a word!

The second decision you must make is how to present the Latin sentences. As your audience probably will not know Latin, they may not understand the meaning unless you clarify it for them. One possibility is simply to state the idea in an English translation, but doing so would mean losing some of the medieval flavor of the piece. Or the character might say the words in Latin and then immediately state the English translation. That might be the best choice for presenting the motto on the coat of arms. Because the last Latin expression, *"In pace requiescat,"* may be more familiar to your audience, you might clarify the meaning by speaking the Latin while crossing yourself in the manner used by people of the Roman Catholic faith. Whatever choice you make, be certain that it is clear and appropriate and that it does not call attention to itself.

Preparing for Presentation

In preparing any prose selection for presentation, you would follow a process of analysis, study, and decision making similar to that suggested for Poe's tale. For most presentations you would also need to write an introduction, one that gives the title of the selection and the author and at the very least provides necessary background for the audience to understand the performance.

Another matter you would consider during preparation time is the use of a folder for the manuscript. Generally, prose performances, whether class assignments or contest events, require that the reader hold and use a script. If you use a script, you must handle it effectively.

And certainly you would need repeated rehearsals in order to put all the elements of the performance together.

Activity 4   Putting It All Together

1. Several prose selections follow. All have been chosen for their appropriateness for young performers. Try working with the techniques discussed in this chapter as you explore these selections.

from WHERE THE RED FERN GROWS
by Wilson Rawls

Rawls' story is told through the eyes of a grown man who remembers growing up in the Ozarks with his parents, his sisters, and his two dogs, Old Dan and Little Ann. After Old Dan dies after a fight with a wildcat, Billy believes he has lost a part of himself. But that is only the start of his lesson about loss and growing up.

Two days later, when I came in from the bottoms where my father and I were clearing land my mother said, "Billy, you had better look after your dog. She won't eat."

I started looking for her. I went to the barn, the corncrib, and looked under the porch. I called her name. It was no use. I rounded up my sisters and asked if they had seen Little Ann. The youngest one said she had seen her go down into the garden. I went there, calling her name. She wouldn't answer my call.

I was about to give up, and then I saw her. She had wiggled her way far back under the thorny limbs of a blackberry bush in the corner of the garden. I talked to her and tried to coax her out. She wouldn't budge. I got down on my knees and crawled back to her. As I did, she raised her head and looked at me.

Her eyes told the story. They weren't the soft gray eyes I had looked into so many times. They were dull and cloudy. There was no fire, no life. I couldn't understand.

I carried her back to the house. I offered her food and water. She wouldn't touch it. I noticed how lifeless she was. I thought perhaps she had a wound I had overlooked. I felt and prodded with my fingers. I could find nothing.

My father came and looked at her. He shook his head and said, "Billy, it's no use. The life has gone out of her. She has no will to live."

He turned and walked away.

I couldn't believe it. I couldn't.

With eggs and rich cream, I made a liquid. I pried her mouth open and poured it down. She responded to nothing I did. I carried her to the porch, and laid her in the same place I had laid the body of Old Dan. I covered her with gunny sacks.

All through the night I would get up and check on her. Next morning I took warm fresh milk and again I opened her mouth and fed her. It was a miserable day for me. At noon it was the same. My dog had just given up. There was no will to live.

That evening when I came in from the fields, she was gone. I hurried to my mother. Mama told me she had seen her go up the hollow from the house, so weak she could hardly stand. Mama had watched her until she had disappeared in the timber.

I hurried up the hollow, calling her name. I called and called. I went up to the head of it, still calling her name and praying she would come to me. I climbed out onto the flats; looking, searching, and calling. It was no use. My dog was gone.

I had a thought, a ray of hope. I just knew I'd find her at the grave of Old Dan. I hurried there.

I found her lying on her stomach, her hind legs stretched out straight, and her front feet folded back under her chest. She had laid her head on his grave. I saw the trail where she had dragged herself through the leaves. The way she lay there, I thought she was alive. I called her name. She made no movement. With the last ounce of strength in her body, she had dragged herself to the grave of Old Dan.

Kneeling down by her side, I reached out and touched her. There was no response, no whimpering cry or friendly wag of her tail. My little dog was dead.

I laid her head in my lap and with tear-filled eyes gazed up into the heavens. In a choking voice, I asked, "Why did they have to die? Why must I hurt so? What have I done wrong?"

I heard a noise behind me. It was my mother. She sat down and put her arm around me.

"You've done no wrong, Billy," she said. "I know this seems terrible and I know how it hurts, but at one time or another, everyone suffers. . . ."

"I know, Mama," I said, "but I can't understand. It was bad enough when Old Dan died. Now Little Ann is gone. Both of them gone, just like that."

"Billy, you haven't lost your dogs altogether," Mama said. "You'll always have their memory. Besides, you can have some more dogs."

I rebelled at this. "I don't want any more dogs," I said. "I won't ever want another dog. . . ."

FROM TO KILL A MOCKINGBIRD

by Harper Lee

In Lee's novel, Jean Louise Finch, better known as Scout, looks back as an adult on her girlhood in Macomb, Alabama, during the 1930s. One of her memories is about her first day of school.

[My brother] Jem condescended to take me to school the first day, a job usually done by one's parents, but Atticus had said Jem would be delighted to show me where my room was. I think some money changed hands in this transaction, for as we trotted around the corner past the Radley Place I head an unfamiliar jingle in Jem's pockets. When we slowed to a walk at the end of the schoolyard, Jem was careful to explain that during school hours I was not to bother him, I was not to approach him with requests to enact a chapter of *Tarzan and the Ant Men,* to embarrass him with references to his private life, or tag along behind him at recess and noon. I was to stick with the first grade and he would stick with the fifth. In short, I was to leave him alone.

"You mean we can't play any more?" I asked.

"We'll do like we always do at home," he said, "but school you'll see—school's different."

It certainly was. Before the first morning was over, Miss Caroline Fisher, our teacher, hauled me up to the front of the room and patted the palm of my hand with a ruler, then she made me stand in the corner until noon.

Miss Caroline was no more than twenty-one. She had bright auburn hair, pink cheeks, and wore crimson fingernail polish. She also wore high-heeled pumps and a red-and-white-striped dress. She looked and smelled like a peppermint drop. She boarded across the street one door down from us in Mrs. Maudie Atkinson's upstairs front room, and when Miss Maudie introduced us to her, Jem was in a haze for days.

Miss Caroline printed her name on the blackboard and said, "This says I am Miss Caroline Fisher. I am from North Alabama, from Winston County." The class murmured apprehensively, should she prove to harbor her share of the peculiarities indigenous to that region. (When Alabama seceded from the Union on January 11, 1861, Winston County seceded from Alabama, and every child in Maycomb County knew it.) North Alabama was full of Liquor Interests, Big Mules, steel companies, Republicans, professors, and other persons of no background.

Miss Caroline began the day by reading us a story about cats. The cats had long conversations with one another, they wore cunning little clothes and lived in a warm house beneath a kitchen stove. By the time Mrs. Cat called the drugstore for an order of chocolate malted mice, the class was wriggling like a bucketful of catawba worms. Miss Caroline seemed unaware that the ragged, denim-shirted and floursack-skirted first grade, most of whom had chopped cotton and fed hogs from the time they were able to walk, were immune to imaginative literature. Miss Caroline came to the end of the story and said, "*Oh,* my, wasn't that nice?"

Then she went to the blackboard and printed the alphabet in enormous square capitals, turned to the class and asked, "Does anybody know what these are?"

Everybody did; most of the first grade had failed it last year.

I suppose she chose me because she knew my name; as I read the alphabet a faint line appeared between her eyebrows, and after making me read most of *My First Reader* and the stock-market quotations from *The Mobile Register* aloud, she discovered that I was literate and looked at me with more than faint distaste. Miss Caroline told me to tell my father not to teach me any more, it would interfere with my reading.

"Teach me?" I said in surprise. "He hasn't taught me anything, Miss Caroline. Atticus ain't got time to teach me anything," I added, when Miss Caroline smiled and shook her head. "Why, he's so tired at night he just sits in the livingroom and reads."

"If he didn't teach you, who did?" Miss Caroline asked good-naturedly. "Somebody did. You weren't born reading *The Mobile Register.*"

"Jem says I was. He read in a book where I was a Bullfinch instead of a Finch. Jem says my name's really Jean Louise Bullfinch, that I got swapped when I was born and I'm really a—"

Miss Caroline apparently thought I was lying. "Let's not let our imaginations run away with us, dear," she said. "Now you tell your father not to teach you any more. It's best to begin reading with a fresh mind. You tell him I'll take over from here and try to undo the damage—"

"Ma'am?"

"Your father does not know how to teach. You can have a seat now."

I mumbled that I was sorry and retired meditating upon my crime.

FROM THE GREAT SANTINI

by Pat Conroy

The Great Santini is the story of Marine Colonel Bull Meecham and his family. The oldest child, Ben, now in high school, is a young man who has learned the discipline demanded by his father. Over the years, the family has moved from place to place, and the Meecham children have had to adjust and make new friends. In the following excerpt from the novel, Ben finds himself in the uncomfortable position of being on a date arranged by his father. To make matters worse, he is driving his father's 1951 Plymouth, a car displaying two large circular decals featuring the grotesquely salivating Werewolf emblem symbolizing the historical ferocity of his father's squadron.

Ben picked up Ansley Matthews at her house on Command Circle, ...

As he saw her, two thoughts occurred to Ben. One was that Ansley was far too pretty for him to date or to consider dating, especially on his first excursion. He felt toadish beneath her gaze. The second was that Ansley had wanted to go on this date even less than he did. Her face was flushed with anger and resignation. She did not speak to either of her parents as they left the house, Ben filling in for the hostile silences by exuberantly bidding the Matthews farewell again and again.

Standing before the glowing decal of the 367 and staring with horror at the dripping fangs of the Werewolf mascot, Ansley put her hands on her hips and shrieked, "I'm not going anywhere with this silly, horrid thing on the side of the car. . . . It's going to be embarrassing enough for me tonight without riding around in this disgusting car."

Ben opened the door to the car, his knees so weak that he seemed likely to collapse in the driveway. "This is the only car I could get tonight, Ansley," he said.

She shook her head, clicked her teeth, and slid into the car. Rounding the car, Ben was trembling so hard he wondered if he would be able to drive.

For five minutes, Ansley refused to speak, ignoring every question he asked. Finally, Ben said, "Look, Ansley. I can take you back home if you want. My father and your father set this date up, you know."

"My father forced me to go," Ansley said. "I have a steady boyfriend."

"I know you have a boyfriend. My father made me go tonight, too. Do you have any particular place you want to go?"

"I don't want to go anywhere in this car. I'd rather die."

"Do you like being a cheerleader?" Ben said, changing the subject and grateful that at least she had begun answering his questions.

"I'd rather cheer than anything in the world," she said, then looking at Ben asked, "Why don't you play football? You're big enough."

"I don't like football."

"You're nothing at this school if you don't play football."

"You don't play football."

"I guess that's supposed to be funny."

"I play basketball."

"Basketball's nothing. An absolute zero. Jim Don plays basketball and that's the only reason I even like to cheer at the games. He's captain of the football team, you know. I never saw you at any of the football games. Where'd you normally sit?"

"I never went to any games."

"Boy, you sure are eaten up with school spirit, aren't you, Ben? My daddy's trying to break me and Jim Don up. But he'll never be able to do it. I just hope Jim Don doesn't see us tonight. He beat up one boy that dated me."

"Oh, that's great," Ben said, instinctively checking the rearview mirror.

"He's insanely jealous. But he's so sweet. I just hope he doesn't see us tonight. He told me he'd be out cruising looking for us."

"We won't go anywhere where he can see us."

"Oh, we have to. We just have to. We have to make the scene at the Shack. My daddy told me to show you where all the gang hangs out. Jim Don has a new Impala. He packed tomatoes last summer and made enough money for a big down payment. Are those Weejuns you're wearing?" she asked Ben.

"What?" Ben asked.

"Weejuns. Loafers. Everyone at the school wears Weejuns."

"No, they're just loafers. I don't know what kind they are."

"That's a Gant shirt, isn't it?"

"It might be. Mom bought it at the PX yesterday."

"No, it's not Gant," she said impatiently. "The PX doesn't sell them and there's no loop at the back."

"It's Ivy League, though," Ben offered. "It's got buttons on the collar."

"That's no big deal . . . ."

Ben turned into the parking lot of the Shack as Ansley slid down in the front seat until her head was not visible to anyone looking in through the driver's side of the car. To his mortification, Ben could see people laughing as they spotted the squadron decals on the side of the car. Choosing the loneliest, most desolate spot he could find, he backed under an overhanging tree in the far corner of the lot.

Only then did Ansley's eyes rise to window level and make a peremptory examination of the other cars.

"You don't mind if I say 'hi' to a few of my friends, Ben. I see some cheerleaders and their boyfriends parked over there under the light. Order me a cheeseburger without onions, a Coca-Cola, medium, and a large order of fries if Lewis comes while I'm gone," she said, blowing him a kiss through the window. She seemed shamelessly gratified to be escaping Ben's presence.

Ben rolled down the window and leaned his elbow on the door.

from I Know Why the Caged Bird Sings

by Maya Angelou

I Know Why the Caged Bird Sings is Angelou's autobiography covering the years of her childhood spent in Stamps, Arkansas. Although prose fiction has been the emphasis in Chapters 3 and 4, autobiographies, biographies, diaries, letters, and commentaries can also make excellent prose readings. This particular selection, the story of a spirited church service, has all the qualities of a work of prose fiction; the difference is that this story happens to be true.

On my way in to church, I saw Sister Monroe, her open-faced gold crown glinting when she opened her mouth to return a neighborly greeting. She lived in the country and couldn't get to church every Sunday, so she made up for her absences by shouting so hard when she did make it that she shook the whole church. As soon as she took her seat, all the ushers would move to her side of the church because it took three women and sometimes a man or two to hold her.

Once when she hadn't been to church for a few months (she had taken off to have a child), she got the spirit and started shouting, throwing her arms around and jerking her body, so that the ushers went over to hold her down, but she tore herself away from them and ran up to the pulpit. She stood in front of the altar, shaking like a freshly caught trout. She screamed at Reverend Taylor. "Preach it. I say, preach it." Naturally he kept on preaching as if she wasn't standing there telling him what to do. Then she screamed an extremely fierce "I said, preach it" and stepped up on the altar. The Reverend kept on throwing out phrases like home-run balls and Sister Monroe made a quick break and grasped for him. For just a second, everything and everyone in the church except Reverend Taylor and Sister Monroe hung loose like stockings on a washline. Then she caught the minister by the sleeve of his jacket and his coattail, then she rocked him from side to side.

I have to say this for our minister, he never stopped giving us the lesson. The usher board made its way to the pulpit, going up both aisles with a little more haste than is customarily seen in church. Truth to tell, they fairly ran to the minister's aid. Then two of the deacons, in their shiny Sunday suits, joined the ladies in white on the pulpit, and each time they pried Sister Monroe loose from the preacher he took another deep breath and kept on preaching, and Sister Monroe grabbed him in another place, and more firmly. Reverend Taylor was helping his rescuers as much as possible by jumping around when he got a chance. His voice at one point got so low it sounded like a roll of thunder, then Sister Monroe's "Preach it" cut through the roar, and we all wondered (I did, in any case) if it would ever end. Would they go on forever, or get tired out at last like a game of blindman's bluff that lasted too long, with nobody caring who was "it"?

I'll never know what might have happened, because magically the pandemonium spread. The spirit infused Deacon Jackson and Sister Willson, the chairman of the usher board, at the same time. Deacon Jackson, a tall, thin, quiet man, who is also a part-time Sunday school teacher, gave a scream like a falling tree, leaned back on thin air and punched Reverend Taylor on the arm. It must have hurt as much as it caught the Reverend unawares. There was a moment's break in the rolling sounds and Reverend Taylor jerked around surprised, and hauled off and punched Deacon Jackson. The same second Sister Willson caught his tie, looped it over her fist a few times, and pressed down on him. There wasn't time to laugh or cry before all three of them were down on the floor behind the altar. Their legs spiked out like kindling wood.

Sister Monroe, who had been the cause of all the excitement, walked off the dais, cool and spent, and raised her flinty voice in the hymn, "I came to Jesus, as I was, worried, wound, and sad, I found in Him a resting place and He has made me glad."

The minister took advantage of already being on the floor and asked in a choky little voice if the church would kneel with him to offer a prayer of thanksgiving. He said we had been visited with a mighty spirit, and let the whole church say Amen.

FROM WHEN THE LEGENDS DIE
by Hal Borland

Hal Borland's novel is the story of a Ute Indian boy named Bear's Brother. Orphaned at age eleven, he has continued to live in the mountains, alone and totally self-sufficient, communing with the wild creatures around him and making a special bond of love with a bear cub he rescued and raised. But then the boy is discovered by the white man administering the nearby Indian reservation, and he is forced to leave his happy existence and go to school, where every attempt is made to reform him. His name changed to Thomas Black Bull, his long braids cut off, his moccasins traded for the boots of the white man, the boy becomes bitter and unhappy. Most of all, he grieves over his separation from the bear he was forced to abandon.

Thomas Black Bull, seeing the tassels on the aspens and the spears on the new grass and the change in the days, sunrise to sunset, knew what time it was in the year. He knew the bears would soon be leaving their winter dens, to travel, to claim their old ranges, to challenge intruders and fight their fearful battles among themselves. He felt these things in his blood.

Then a moonlit night came and he sat in his room and knew what was going to happen. He hoped it would happen, and he wished it would not happen. He waited, and the cattle bawled in their pens. The horses snorted and raced about their corrals. He opened his window, and in the moonlight he saw the bear beside the horse-breaking pen. It stood there nosing in the air, then shuffled its feet like a great shaggy dog and nosed in the air again. It whined softly.

Other windows opened. Someone shouted an alarm.

Thomas picked up a heavy quirt and hurried from his room. He went down the hallway, down the stairs and out into the moonlight. He ran toward the corral, and he began singing the bear song.

The bear came to meet him.

He stopped singing and shouted warning words, then angry words. The bear stopped and growled, then came on, whining again. The boy screamed at the bear in Ute. It stopped again and the boy went up to it, swished the quirt in its face and shouted, "Go away! Go back home, to the mountains!"

The bear rose on its hind legs and spread its forepaws as though to tear the boy to pieces. Its teeth were white in the moonlight. It was a two-year-old now and stood taller than the boy. The boy lashed it across the face with the quirt, again and again, screaming, "Go! Go! Go!"

The bear dropped to all fours, whimpering. It nosed the boy's hands, and it cried like a child. And the boy dropped the quirt, put an arm around its neck, buried his face in its fur and wept. He wept until the bear drew away and licked his face and whimpered and licked his face again.

The boy backed away. "I do not know you!" he cried. "You are no longer my brother. I have no brother! I have no friends!" Then he said, "I had a brother. But when I went to find him and sang my song to my brother he would not listen. Now there is nobody."

He stood silent in the moonlight, his head bowed, and the bear swayed from side to side, from foot to foot, moaning.

"Go away," the boy said. "Go, or they will kill you. They do not need guns to kill. They kill without guns. Listen! I speak the truth. They will kill you. Go away!"

The bear still stood swaying, moaning.

He put a hand in the fur on the bear's neck and he said, "Come. I will go a little way with you." And they slowly walked away from the horse-breaking pen, the boy and the bear in the moonlight. They walked across the grounds toward the aspens with catkins like chipmunk tails. They walked among the trees and into the shadows, and after a little while there was the sound of the sorrow song. It was a song so desolate that the coyotes answered it from the gullies beyond. But the coyote cries were not so full of wailing as that song. The coyotes have brothers.

After another little while the boy came back out of the shadows of the trees, walking alone. He walked with the weariness of one who sings the going-away song for the only other person in the world. But he sang no song.

Men and boys were standing beside the doorway, but he seemed not to see them. They stepped aside, made way for him, and later they said it was like seeing a strange man, a remote and terrible man, not a boy.

He walked past them and along the hallway and upstairs to his room.

The next day he went to his classes as though nothing had happened, but those who looked into his eyes saw something there that made them afraid to talk to him. Nobody spoke of what had happened in the moonlight.

2. Select one of the previous passages, analyze it, write an introduction, practice your vocal and physical delivery, and then interpret the literature for an audience.

3. Make your own selection of a prose reading to perform. Work within a maximum time limit of seven minutes, including introduction. Go through all parts of the process as you analyze, rehearse, and prepare the performance. Then present your interpretation for an audience. ■

5 Analyzing Poetry

Imagine for a Moment . . .

You are sitting in your room listening to your favorite radio station. The melody of a new song begins, one you haven't heard before. What captures your attention first is the beat of the drums. Then the lyrics start, fitting into the pattern set by the drums. As you listen to the words, vivid pictures come to life. You are carried away into the imaginative vision of the performance. Then, after the song, it's time for a commercial:

My bologna has a first name, it's O-S-C-A-R.
My bologna has a second name, it's M-A-Y-E-R.
I like to eat it every day, and if you ask me why
I'll say,
'Cause Oscar Mayer has a way with B-O-L-O-G-N-A.

© *Oscar Mayer Foods Corporation. Oscar Mayer is a registered trademark of Oscar Mayer Foods Corporation.*

The words are clever. The rhythm is easy to follow. And the sounds harmonize.

In both the song and the jingle, you heard the message. But it was the presentation that made the message grab you. In each instance, tools of the poet came into play to catch your interest. In the same way, the interpreter of poetry can excite and hold the attention of an audience by creating rhythm and sound harmonies as part of the interpretation.

Think about these questions:

- When is rhythm in written words more apparent—when you read silently or when you say the words out loud?

- Why is it easier to memorize a short jingle than the words of an ordinary sentence?

The answer to the first question is easy. While you may be aware that words fall into a rhythm when you read them silently, you are more conscious of the beat when you speak the words aloud. Why? Because the voice has the power to give light or heavy stress to spoken words.

And why is it easier to memorize a jingle? Look at the following sentences.

> Red is a popular color for roses, and blue seems appropriate for violets.
> Sugar has a flavor akin to the wonderful sweetness you yourself possess.

Now look at the same idea as you've heard it in jingle form.

> Roses are red.
> Violets are blue.
> Sugar is sweet,
> And so are you!

Because the words in a jingle follow a pattern—that is, have rhythm—and usually rhyme, they set quickly in the mind. Rhythm and rhyme catch attention.

This chapter and the next will examine the tools and techniques of the poet—elements with which you will need familiarity as an interpreter. But remember the various areas of analysis presented in earlier chapters because with poetry, too, you must know who is speaking, who is listening, and what is happening.

Poetry, a Definition

Defining poetry, as with defining prose, is challenging. Poet W. H. Auden describes poetry as "memorable speech." William Wordsworth calls it "the spontaneous overflow of powerful feelings." In terms of setting up a comparison with prose, perhaps professor Laurence Perrine provides the most helpful distinction when he suggests that "**poetry** might be defined as a kind of language that says *more* and says it *more intensely* than does ordinary language."

The heart of poetry, as with any literature, is what it has to say, what it communicates. However, in order to present an effective interpretation, you must understand the basic technical elements that give the poem its shape. These elements include **rhythm, rhyme, and sound harmonies.** Just as carpenters use different tools for different functions so that they can construct a building, poets draw from their collection of tools to construct a poem. Only as you acquire a working knowledge of these tools will you be able to build a truly effective interpretation.

Also understand that the analysis of these elements is not an exact science. There is room for variation. Just look at the structure of a poem, study it, make some decisions about it, and then use the resulting insight to gain control of form so that your oral presentation can recreate the rhythmic and harmonic excitement built into the literature.

Rockin' Rhythm

For a moment, think of times—other than when you listen to music or to jingles—that you are aware of rhythm. When you hear a clock, when you listen to your own heart, when you watch people walk or swim—the list could go on and on. You are surrounded by a variety of rhythms. Poetry imitates these rhythms by placing words in patterns.

How do you say each of the following words?

mother	father	springtime
drinking	impossible	funny

Do you give the same stress, the same emphasis to each syllable? Which syllable receives the stronger emphasis when you say each word?

For *MOTHer, FATHer, SPRINGtime, DRINKing* and *FUNny,* the first syllable receives the heavier emphasis. For the four-syllable word *im-POS-si-ble,* the strongest emphasis is on the second syllable. Now say the word *mother* putting the emphasis on the second syllable. Does your pronunciation sound strange? Try reading the following sentence giving the greater emphasis to the part of the word that is underlined.

MothER hurRIED homeWARD quickLY.

Clearly, when you change the natural way you say words, you distort the way the words should sound.

A poet arranges words so that the natural pronunciation creates a kind of rhythm. Each syllable of every word plays a part in creating a particular poem's flow. Sometimes that rhythm falls into a definite, repeated metrical pattern. Sometimes no repeated pattern exists, but there is almost always an underlying, connecting rhythm that is essential to the poem. Three terms used to identify poetry by its rhythmic structure are **rhymed verse,** which refers to poetry having end-rhyme and a repeated metrical pattern; **blank verse,** which refers to poetry written in unrhymed lines of iambic pentameter; and **free verse,** which refers to poetry having no repeated pattern to its rhythm.

In poetry, a **foot** is a patterned unit of poetic rhythm. That rhythm is measured in terms of **meter,** which comes from a word meaning "to measure." There are four common types of poetic feet.

The **iambic foot** is made up of an unaccented—lightly stressed—syllable followed by an accented—heavily stressed—syllable.

Example: begin

The reverse of the iambic is the **trochaic foot,** which is made up of an accented syllable followed by an unaccented syllable.

Example: after

The **anapestic foot** consists of two unaccented syllables followed by an accented syllable.

Example: understand

And the reverse of the anapestic is the **dactylic foot,** an accented syllable followed by two unaccented syllables.

Example: whispering

Of the poetic feet, the iambic is the most frequently used because it most closely resembles the flow of normal English speech. The dactylic is the least used. Most poems have variation where types of poetic feet are mixed in some lines. Two special types of poetic feet also used for variation are the **pyrrhic foot**—two unaccented syllables coming back to back—and the **spondaic foot**—two accented syllables coming back to back.

Look at the following lines of poetry with the poetic feet marked.

I will not play at tug 'o war
I'd rather play at hug 'o war

Shel Silverstein

́ ˘ | ́   ˘ | ́   ˘ | ́
Over stones and twigs and holes,
́ ˘ | ́   ˘ | ́   ˘ | ́
Over mud and sticks and poles,

Myra Cohn Livingston

˘ ˘   ́ | ˘ ˘   ́
If you look in your soup
˘ ˘   ́ | ˘   ˘   ́
Better hope you don't spy
˘ ́ | ˘   ˘   ́
A fuzzy gray worm
˘ ˘ ́ | ˘   ˘   ́
Or a buzzing black fly.

Jere Aston

́   ́ | ˘   ́ | ́   ˘
Snow falling, roads freezing,
́   ́ | ˘   ́ | ́   ˘
Lips chapping, nose sneezing,

William Dean

́ ˘ | ˘   ˘ | ́   ́
Slowly in the dark night
́   ˘ | ́   ˘ | ́   ˘
Moonlight slips between the
́   ˘ | ́   ˘ | ́   ́
Clouds to make the earth bright.

Anne Warren

Notice that when you indicate poetic feet, you mark each syllable that is pronounced. Some words have only one syllable. Some have several. A line of poetry is measured by the number of poetic feet that are in it. Marking the rhythm and dividing the lines into poetic feet is called **scanning.** Here are some basic rules to help you find the proper way to refer to the meter of a poem.

If a line contains one poetic foot, the line is **monometer.**

If a line contains two poetic feet, the line is **dimeter.**

If a line contains three poetic feet, the line is **trimeter.**

If a line contains four poetic feet, the line is **tetrameter.**

If a line contains five poetic feet, the line is **pentameter.**

If a line contains six poetic feet, the line is **hexameter.**

If a line contains seven poetic feet, the line is **heptameter.**

If a poem is written in lines containing four dactylic feet, then the **metrical structure** is *dactylic tetrameter.* If it is written in lines each containing one iambic foot, then the metrical structure is *iambic monometer.*

Activity 1   Identifying Rhythm and Meter

1. Go back to the quoted lines and read each aloud several times listening to the flow of the rhythm as it is marked.

2. Identify the type of poetic foot used predominantly in the lines.

3. Look through the lines and find any variation from the predominant poetic foot. Identify the type of poetic foot used for variation. The lines from the poem by Anne Warren have the most variation.

4. Examine each set of lines and decide whether it represents dimeter, trimeter, or tetrameter structure. ■

Knowing what scanning is and understanding how meter works are important. But an interpreter does not have to be an expert scanner, devoting hours to marking rhythmic structures. After all, there is not just one correct way to decide which syllables are stressed and which are unstressed. Your job is to be aware of rhythm and its importance. For instance, the more stressed syllables in a given line, the slower that line will usually move. See how the last line of the Warren poem on the previous page is slowed by the heavy stresses. Lines that rely on iambic and anapestic feet—often called **rising rhythms**—also tend to move more slowly than lines using trochaic and dactylic feet—**falling rhythms.** To create a sense of stateliness, then, a poet might choose a rising rhythm for the slowness. To suggest a quick motion or to create humor, on the other hand, the poet might choose a faster falling rhythm. Notice how in the line below, the anapestic foot helps suggest the movement of a galloping horse.

Through the desert he galloped at war with the wind.

The impact of rhythm comes from the way it works on emotions, heightening awareness as it sends signals about mood and meaning. Therefore, marking the rhythm can be a good way to gain insight into a particular poem. You'll find the more you work with meter, the easier scanning becomes.

One discovery you will make as you work through a poem is that even though meter is measured by the line, meaning doesn't always stop at the end of the line. **Enjambment** is the term used to indicate that one line of poetry must run into another to complete its meaning. In poetry, meaning often flows through several lines. Don't get so caught up in the rhythm of a poem that you let it dictate where you pause. Keep your focus on the meaning that the rhythm supports, allowing that meaning to guide you in responding to the rhythm.

Many poems are divided into sections or groups of lines called **stanzas**. Since stanza division isn't an element that stands out when a poem is read aloud, your concern as an interpreter is to be aware of how the stanzas work together to build the total poem. Only then can you use that knowledge to make choices about vocal delivery.

Activity 2   Reading Rhythm and Meter

1. Study the following poems. Examine the metrical structures of each and become familiar with the rhythm of the lines. On a separate sheet of paper, try marking the syllables you would accent and those that would receive lighter stress.

SEA GULL

The sea gull curves his wings,
the sea gull turns his eyes.
Get down into the water, fish!
(if you are wise.)

The sea gull slants his wings,
the sea gull turns his head.
Get deep into the water, fish!
(or you'll be dead.)

Elizabeth Coatsworth

Deer Hunt

Because the warden is a cousin, my
mountain friends hunt in summer when the deer
cherish each rattler-ridden spring, and I
have waited hours by a pool in fear
that manhood would require I shoot or that
the steady drip of the hill would dull my ear
to a snake whispering near the log I sat
upon, and listened to the yelping cheer
of dogs and men resounding ridge to ridge.
I flinched at every lonely rifle crack,
my knuckles whitening where I gripped the edge
of age and clung, like retching, sinking back,
then gripping once again the monstrous gun—
since I, to be a man, had taken one.

Judson Jerome

2. Read both poems aloud. For the first reading, pause at the end of each line as though the line could stand alone. You might find a partner and take turns reading aloud to each other, pausing at the end of each line. Does stopping at the end of each line work for both poems? How do the two poems differ? Now return to the second poem and reread it aloud. This time pause only where punctuation would indicate the need for a pause. Does the rhythm flow smoothly? Does the meaning hold together better? What have you discovered about the way poetic lines are constructed? ■

Time for Rhyme

Another structural element important to poetry is **rhyme,** the occurrence of the same stressed vowel sound and all succeeding sounds in two or more words such as *light/night/bright, sun/ one,* and *mister/blister/sister.* When only one syllable is involved in the rhyme, as in *kiss/ miss,* the rhyme is called **masculine.** *Ringing/singing* is an example of **feminine rhyme,** which occurs when the rhyming word ends on an unaccented syllable. Though not all poetry relies on rhyme, much poetry does, depending on it to unify structure and to create a musical effect.

The word **rhyme scheme** refers to the pattern into which rhyme falls when it occurs at the ends of lines. In the poem "Sea Gull," for instance, the words at the ends of the second and fourth lines of each stanza rhyme. The rhymed words are *eyes/wise, head/dead;* and the rhyme scheme would be written ***abcb defe.*** The rhyme scheme of each stanza is written separately using a lowercase letter to represent each possible rhyme sound. When two words rhyme, the same letter is used to indicate the rhyme. In "Sea Gull" the rhymed words stand out distinctly.

Now, silently, read the poem "Deer Hunt." On a separate piece of paper, jot down the rhyme scheme. To get you started, note the first line would get the letter *a;* the second line, *b.* Since the third line ends with a word that rhymes with "my," the third line would get the letter *a*, and so on. Be aware of how rhyme works in this poem and that there may be a difference in how each person records the rhyme scheme for this particular poem, depending on if that person thinks the words "ridge" and "edge" rhyme. Now read "Deer Hunt" aloud. Notice how the lines flow together because of the poem's structure and how the rhyme scheme becomes less obvious.

As an individual interpreter, you may enjoy the challenge of working with rhymed verse because of the musicality created by its rhythm and rhyme. On the other hand, you may come to feel that poetry that is more subtle in its rhythm is easier for you to work with and control. There exists a large body of poetry, especially modern poetry, that avoids the use of repeated meter and rhyme altogether.

Free verse poetry that does not have a clearly repeated pattern to its rhythm or rhyme scheme can be a good choice for an interpreter who finds himself or herself falling into a sing-song vocal pattern when interpreting rhymed verse. Yet even free verse, as in the next activity, generally has a rhythmic flow that you will need to discover and control.

Activity 3 Playing with Rhythm and Rhyme

1. Study the following poem. Examine the way the lines flow together. Notice that there is no repeated rhyme and no repeated pattern to the rhyme.

ARITHMETIC

Arithmetic is where numbers fly
    like pigeons in and out of your head.
Arithmetic tells you how many you lose or win
    if you know how many you had
    before you lost or won.
Arithmetic is seven eleven all good children
    go to heaven—or five six bundle of sticks.
Arithmetic is numbers you squeeze from your
    head to your hand to your pencil to your paper
    till you get the right answer. . . .
If you have two animal crackers, one good and one bad,
    and you eat one and a striped zebra
    with streaks all over him eats the other,
    how many animal crackers will you have
    if somebody offers you five six seven and you say
    No no no and you say Nay nay nay
    and you say Nix nix nix?
If you ask your mother for one fried egg
    for breakfast and she gives you
    two fried eggs and you eat
    both of them, who is better in arithmetic,
    you or your mother?

                                                    Carl Sandburg

2. Read the poem aloud. You might find a partner and take turns reading aloud to each other. Does the poem flow smoothly? Do you get a definite sense of rhythm as you read or hear the poem? Are there places where rhyme is used? Find all the rhyme. Notice that sometimes words within a line rhyme or a word at the end of one line rhymes with a word in the middle of that line or another line. This kind of rhyme is called **internal rhyme**. ■

Other Sound Harmonies

Along with end rhyme and internal rhyme, a number of other tools are available to create sound harmony. Because the interpreter reads aloud, these harmonies become an integral part of the interpretation.

Look again at "Arithmetic." See where Sandburg repeats "No no no," "Nay nay nay," and "Nix nix nix." **Repetition** can be an effective tool. It creates a kind of word echo. It also can create a specific beat. Here the short words come back to back, bringing together three accented words to play within the rhythm. Go back and read that section of the poem again and see how the words play against each other. Try reading the section fast. Then go slowly. Which produces the better results for you? Why?

Another tool is **alliteration,** the repetition of an initial consonant sound in several words close together. Sometimes the alliteration will work in conjunction with another device, **consonance,** the repetition of a consonant sound within words close together. Look at the following short humorous poem.

FREDDY

Here is the story
Of Freddy, my friend,
Who ran out in traffic
And that is the end.

Dennis Lee

In this four-line poem, it's possible to see a variety of sound harmonies reacting together. The consonants *r, s,* and *f* demonstrate how alliteration and consonance complement one another to create a sense of fluid unity. The short *a* and the short *i* in the last two lines illustrate **assonance,** the repetition of the same vowel sound surrounded by different consonant sounds. They, too, create a bond in sound.

An interpreter needs to become comfortable with the way sound harmonies function because they contribute to the poem's musicality as the words are spoken. Brain research suggests that these sounds connect with and excite the right side of the brain. That's one way they can help you enchant an audience. Examine the line:

See the snake that poses hissing.

The *s* sound used alliteratively in *see* and *snake* appears again in *poses* and *hissing.* The consonance functions with the alliteration so that there is a suggestion of the hissing sound a snake makes before it strikes. As you read the line to an audience, the left brain of each listener may know that the snake "poses"; it will be the right brain, however, that hears the unnerving hissing.

The word *hissing* also illustrates **onomatopoeia,** the use of a word that suggests the sound of the word itself. An old Alka-Seltzer advertising jingle announced:

PLOP, PLOP, FIZZ, FIZZ,
OH WHAT A RELIEF IT IS!

Courtesy of Miles Inc., Pittsburgh.

The words *plop* and *fizz* demonstrate onomatopoeia in action. Sound helps the image come to life. Other onomatopoeic words include *buzz, murmur, wheeze,* and *rattle.* Imagine the way you can play such harmonic devices in your performance.

The Connection of Meaning and Sound

What makes the reading of poetry demanding on the interpreter is discovering how meaning and sound function together. A poet may have an experience to share, a nerve to expose, a portrait to paint, or perhaps a story to tell. But in the sharing, exposing, painting, or telling, the poet tries to support and reinforce the meaning with the poetic tools available. How are these ends accomplished?

Sometimes the poet controls speed and movement of lines to indicate the progression of feeling or a specific action suggested by the words. Look at the following stanza from a poem by Henry Wadsworth Longfellow.

> ˘ ´ | ´ ˘ | ˘ ˘ ´
> The tide rises, the tide falls,
> ˘ ´ | ˘ ´ | ˘ ˘ ´ | ˘ ´
> The twilight darkens, the curlew calls;
> ˘ ˘ ´ | ˘ ´ | ˘ ´ | ˘ ´
> And along the sea-sands damp and brown
> ˘ ´ | ˘ ˘ ´ | ˘ ˘ | ˘ ´
> The traveler hastens toward the town.
> ˘ ˘ ´ | ´ ˘ | ˘ ˘ ´
> And the tide rises, the tide falls.

The rhythm clearly suggests the flow of the tide, an effect created primarily by using a dactylic foot to interrupt two iambic feet in line 1 and by playing that same dactylic beat against an anapestic and an iambic foot in the last line. Except for the falling rhythm of these two dactylic feet, the rest of the poem relies on a rising rhythm. At the same time, the long *i* sound in *tide* and *rises* in the first and last lines creates a soft harmony in the middle of the lines for the contrasting sound of the word *falls* to play against. And throughout the stanza, the *s* sound unifies the flowing motion. The poet is using the harmony to underscore the meaning. Notice, too, how "curlew calls" suggests the very sound made by the long-beaked seabird.

What Longfellow does is not accidental. As a poet he has made conscious choices about how to arrange and use words to enhance what he has to say.

Activity 4   Preparing for Performance

1. Study the following poem. Identify the rhyme scheme as well as examples of repetition, alliteration, consonance, assonance, and onomatopoeia. What role do these elements play in enhancing the overall flow of the poem? How do they help to emphasize and clarify what the poem is saying? Would the poem be as effective without the use of these various devices? As an interpreter of the poem, how can you use the devices to assist you with your performance?

WE'RE RACING, RACING DOWN THE WALK

We're racing, racing down the walk,
Over the pavement and round the block.
We rumble along till the sidewalk ends—
Felicia and I and half our friends
Our hair flies backward. It's whish and whirr!

She roars at me and I shout at her
As past the porches and garden gates
We rattle and rock
On roller skates.

Phyllis McGinley

2. Find two poems that excite your interest in some way. You might look in your literature textbook or go to the library to find a book of poems. Once you make your selections, examine the technical aspects of the poem—the rhythm, rhyme, and other devices of sound that wake up its basic structure. Decide what each tool contributes to the poem and how you might work with it to assist you in creating your interpretation.

3. Now prepare to present a reading of one of the poems. Be ready to explain how your analysis of structure assisted in your preparation. ■

6 Poetry, from Printed Page to Performance

Your Assignment Is . . .

Think about a baked turkey, dressing, cranberry sauce, sweet potatoes, and pumpkin pie. Imagine the food sitting on a table decorated by a cornucopia filled with Indian corn and dried gourds. What holiday comes to mind? Your immediate answer is probably Thanksgiving, and the reason is that all the elements mentioned point toward that one holiday.

As an interpreter, you want all the elements of your reading to come together to create the same kind of complete picture. To do that, you have to make the tools of poetic structure serve the purpose of helping you give life to your reading. You have to pull together rhythm, rhyme, image, emotion, and theme as you use your voice and bodily action to communicate.

In Chapter 5 you dealt with rhythm and rhyme. Now look at image. An **image** is a group of words that capture a sense impression. The words work together to create a verbal impression of something the poet wants you to see, hear, feel, taste, or smell. As an interpreter, you want your audience to share those same sensations.

Examine the poem "The Great Figure" by William Carlos Williams.

Among the rain
and lights
I saw the figure 5
in gold
on a red
firetruck
moving
tense
unheeded
to gong clangs
siren howls
and wheels rumbling
through the dark city.

All words work together to suggest a specific impression—the image of a fire truck moving noisily down a dark, wet street.

Figures of speech can help create images. Think about the following expressions. What does each one mean?

"I need some wheels."

"Hit the books."

"Chill out."

Although each expression has a literal meaning, the actual meaning is figurative. To need some wheels, for instance, suggests the desire for a car, not just four tires. Hitting the books doesn't really mean to slam a fist against a pile of texts. The expression means to attack the books mentally, to study. And "chill out" implies calming down emotionally rather than cooling off physically.

Figures of Speech

Here is a review of some of the most often used figures of speech—expressions that transcend the literal to create a specific word picture.

- A **metaphor** is a comparison of unlike things. But more than just comparing, it actually transforms one thing into another. A metaphor is a kind of shorthand, densely packed with meaning.

    The sun, the golden eye of day
    [The sun becomes a golden eye.]

    My life became a dying fire.
    [Life is called a dying fire, probably indicating the later years.]

- A **simile** is a figure of speech making a direct comparison by using *like* or *as*.

    He attacked like a tiger.
    [A person's fighting skill is compared to that of a tiger.]

    Her voice as gentle as the rain
    [The quality of a speaker's voice is compared to soft rain.]

- **Personification** grants human qualities to things that are not human, enabling a kind of empathy with inanimate objects.

    The wind cried out in anger.
    [The wind is given the human quality of crying angrily.]

    The rocks themselves began to speak,
    And the flowers whirled in a dance.
    [The rocks are given the human quality of speaking, and the flowers have the human movement of dance.]

- **Symbolism** results when an object, action, person, or situation is used to represent an idea larger than itself. The color white, for example, can be used to represent purity or innocence; and the heart is a popular symbol for love. Poets often rely on symbolic language to expand meaning, for the symbol calls to mind a broader context than literal language.

- The **hyperbole** is an overstatement, a deliberate exaggeration of reality enlarging the impact of what is being said.

The shot heard round the world
[This phrase was used to describe the firing of the bullet that started the American Revolution. The exaggeration indicates that the effect of the shot shook the whole world.]

A river of blood gushed from his side.
[The exaggeration turns a stream of blood into a gushing river.]

- **Litotes** is a specific kind of understatement which expresses an affirmative position through a negative statement.

    His victory was no small feat.
    [The understating of the victory actually serves to play up its magnitude.]

    A bee sting brings little comfort.
    [Saying that a sting brings little comfort emphasizes the idea that the sting causes pain.]

- An **allusion** is a reference to a person, place, or event from classical literature, history, or the Bible, expanding the literal meaning of what is being said.

    Remember the Alamo!
    [Unless you know what happened at the Alamo, the statement has no meaning.]

    A new Achilles
    Strong yet weak
    At once.
    [Unless you know who the original Achilles was and understand that he was invulnerable except for his heel, then your picture of this "new Achilles" will be incomplete.]

- **Synecdoche** makes use of a part to represent the whole, focusing on a specific aspect of the event or experience being described.

    His pedaling feet
    Carried him down the street.
    [It wasn't just pedaling feet but the entire bicycle ridden by the entire person that moved down the street.]

- An **apostrophe** is the addressing of someone absent or something not human as if it were alive and present and could, if it so desired, respond. An apostrophe can suggest immediacy.

    O Cloud, my distant confidante, I call to you.
    [The cloud is addressed directly, as though it could hear and answer.]

- An **oxymoron** places two seemingly contradictory words or elements back to back to create a striking image and imply different meanings for the same experience or feeling.

    Loud silence shouting to the hills
    [*Loud* and *silence* suggest opposite extremes that create a vivid image when the words are placed side by side.]

    Beautiful tyrant! fiend angelical!
    [This line from Shakespeare's play *Romeo and Juliet*, spoken by Juliet when she learns that Romeo has killed her cousin Tybalt, shows her ambivalent feelings: Romeo is both *beautiful* and *tyrannical*; he's a *fiend* and an *angel*.]

Overall, figurative language helps to make the abstract concrete, increases the emotional intensity of what is being said, and compresses ideas. Like individual words, figurative language can be multidimensional; and such expressions are pleasurable to hear because they have the power to excite the senses.

Activity 1 Finding Word Pictures

1. Read the following poem by Janell Howard. After several readings, close your eyes and allow the words to give you a mental picture. Then describe that picture in your own words.

A LOVER'S TOY

O box, black box, as hard and cold as stone,
You sit in ghost-like silence by my bed
Where I recline in agony alone.

O ugly plastic mass with wires for soul,
I beg for you to ring and bring his voice
To touch my breaking heart and make it whole.

But you, you do not hear my whispered prayer;
Your dull, dark face just stares with no response
To reach into the depth of my despair.

How heedless, cold, and black that careless boy
Who played with stark indifference on my heart,
As though it were, like you, a lover's toy.

2. Go back through the poem and pick out specific figures of speech that help create the picture you see. How do these figures of speech function together to excite your senses? ■

Types of Poetry

Now that you are familiar with the elements that give a poem shape, texture, and color, you need to look at poems in terms of content. Three content types that provide excellent material for interpretation are **narrative, lyric,** and **dramatic.**

Narrative poetry presents a story in verse form. The elements of a story—plot, character, setting, for example—are of primary importance. "Paul Revere's Ride" by Henry Wadsworth Longfellow, "Casey at the Bat" by Ernest Lawrence Thayer, "The Cremation of Sam Magee" by Robert Service, and "Death of the Hired Man" by Robert Frost are well-known examples of narrative poems.

Lyric poetry deals specifically with the emotions and the senses. It is the most intense and personal form of poetry. There may be some elements that appear to be narrative, but these are secondary to the lyrical elements of the poem. "A Lover's Toy," for example, is lyric. Certainly, the poem tells you that a boy has ended his relationship with a girl; but the poem does not reveal a fully developed story. Rather it focuses on the feelings, the emotions, of the girl. Two other examples of lyric poetry—Judson Jerome's "Deer Hunt" and Carl Sandburg's "Arithmetic"—appear in Chapter 5.

Dramatic poetry, as the name implies, makes specific use of techniques associated with drama. There is generally a speaker who communicates in a soliloquy or monologue. A dramatic situation is either implied or stated. Examples of dramatic poetry are Robert Browning's "Porphyria's Lover," included at the end of this chapter, Alfred Lord Tennyson's "Ulysses," and Edgar Lee Masters' *Spoon River Anthology.* Three of Masters' poems appear in Chapter 1.

Plays written in verse form represent a type of dramatic poetry, but because the poetry is part of an overall play, there is general agreement that poetry taken from a play should not be used for poetry interpretation. For instance, Hamlet's famous soliloquy beginning with

60   Getting Started in Oral Interpretation the words "To be or not to be" is wonderfully poetic; however, it is part of a drama rather than an individual poem.

Becoming aware of types of poetry can help you decide where to place the focus when preparing and performing your interpretation. Elements of the story—characterization and plot, for instance—might be your focus with a narrative poem, while general mood might be the focus with a lyric poem. However, being able to identify poetic type is only part of an overall process. The final product of that process should be a meaningful oral reading.

Putting the Preparation Process to Work

Pretend your assignment is to prepare a three-minute interpretation of a poem. Karl Shapiro's "Auto Wreck" nicely fits the bill. Read the poem to yourself.

AUTO WRECK

Its quick soft silver bell beating, beating,
And down the dark one ruby flare
Pulsing out red light like an artery,
The ambulance at top speed floating down
Past beacons and illuminated clocks
Wings in a heavy curve, dips down,
And brakes speed, entering the crowd.
The doors leap open, emptying light;
Stretchers are laid out, the mangled lifted
And stowed into the little hospital.
Then the bell, breaking the hush, tolls once,
And the ambulance with its terrible cargo
Rocking, slightly rocking, moves away,
As the doors, an afterthought, are closed.

We are deranged, walking among the cops
Who sweep glass and are large and composed.
One is still making notes under the light.
One with a bucket douches ponds of blood
Into the street and gutter.
One hangs lanterns on the wrecks that cling,
Empty husks of locusts, to iron poles.

Our throats were tight as tourniquets,
Our feet were bound with splints, but now
Like convalescents intimate and gauche,
We speak through sickly smiles and warn
With stubborn saw of common sense,
The grim joke and the banal resolution.
The traffic moves around with care,
But we remain, touching a wound
That opens to our richest horror.

Already old, the question Who shall die?
Becomes unspoken Who is innocent?
For death in war is done by hands;
Suicide has cause and stillbirth, logic.
But this invites the occult mind,
Cancels our physics with a sneer,
And spatters all we knew of denouement
Across the expedient and wicked stones.

Normally, 110 to 120 words a minute represents a good reading speed. A quick count of Shapiro's poem shows there are 251 words, so that would suggest a reading time of a little over two minutes. Add a 30 to 45 second introduction, and that would make a three-minute presentation.

Counting words will not always give an exact timing for a poem, however, or for a prose or drama selection for that matter; so it's best for you to read the material aloud to check the time. Remember, counting words doesn't account for dramatic pauses; nor does it take into consideration slowing down or speeding up because of demands in the literature.

One approach to analyzing the poem, or any work of literature, would be to establish and then answer a series of questions about the selection you are preparing for interpretation. If you find you work better when you have a set of guidelines, then you might find the following questions helpful as you analyze "Auto Wreck."

- What kind of poem are you dealing with? Is it lyric, narrative, or dramatic?

Looking at "Auto Wreck," you might be inclined to say narrative. However, after you go through the poem carefully, you'll see that while some story elements exist, the poem doesn't really develop a well-plotted tale. Instead, it deals with the senses that are heightened as a result of the wreck. You hear the sounds; you see the sights; you feel the tension. The poem is an emotional response to an auto accident rather than a story about that accident. Therefore, it is a lyric poem.

- What is the poet saying in the poem? What does she or he want the reader/listener to experience, feel, or discover?

Shapiro is taking you inside the feelings of someone witnessing the aftermath of a wreck. The speaker begins by reporting what he or she sees, then talks about the feelings the events call forth. Finally, the witness of the accident delves into questioning why such horrible accidents occur; but there is no answer. There is only an empty knowing, an uneasy sensing of the reality. Auto wrecks, like so many things in our lives, seem to lie beyond explanation.

As you explore content to understand the poem, look up any words you do not understand. For example, unless you can define the words "gauche" [line 24], "occult" [line 35], "physics" [line 36], and "denouement" [line 37], you won't be able to give a clear interpretation.

If you are not familiar with one or more of these words, or any other words in the poem, get a dictionary now and look up the meanings.

- Who is the speaker or **persona** in the poem?

An almost automatic response to this question is that the poet is the speaker. The poet is indeed the writer of the lines, and in that respect is the speaker. However, when you interpret a poem you need to decide as specifically as possible who is speaking the words you will be reading. Knowing that persona will help you establish a specific vantage point from which to share what the poem is saying.

Think of some possibilities for the speaker of this poem. The persona could be the driver of a passing car—male or female—who has stopped. Perhaps the speaker is not the driver, but a passenger in a car that has stopped or even in one of the cars involved in the accident. Or maybe the persona is someone who was out walking and came upon the accident.

As you determine the speaker, be as detailed as you can be. Think about the age and personality of the person and decide what relationship he or she has to the accident. These decisions will help you give the spoken words clear meaning.

Remember that in poetry, as in prose, you must be aware that the speaker represents a particular point of view; he or she has motivations and intentions. Discovering what they are is essential in your preparation. Otherwise, there will be no clear reason for any of the actions.

Once you get an overall understanding of the type, point, and persona of the poem, examine the technical elements to see exactly how they relate to what you've already discovered.

- How is the poem put together structurally?

"Auto Wreck" is divided into four stanzas. The word *down* is repeated at the end of lines 4 and 6. The word *closed* at the end of the first stanza rhymes with *composed* in the second line of the second stanza, but other than these possibilities, there is no apparent rhyme scheme.

The rhythm pattern is not regular, nor is it repetitive. The following lines have the metrical structure marked.

> ˘ ´ | ˘ ´ | ˘ ´ | ´ ˘ | ´ ˘
> Its quick soft silver bell beating, beating,
>
> ˘ ´ | ˘ ´ | ˘ ´ | ˘ ´
> And down the dark one ruby flare
>
> ´ ˘ | ˘ ´ | ´ ˘ | ˘ ´ | ˘ ´
> Pulsing out red light like an artery,
>
> ˘ ´ | ˘ ´ | ˘ ´ | ´ ´ | ˘ ´
> The ambulance at top speed floating down
>
> ˘ ´ | ˘ ˘ ˘ ´ | ˘ ´
> Past beacons and illuminated clocks
>
> ´ ˘ | ˘ ´ | ˘ ´ | ˘ ´
> Wings in a heavy curve, dips down,
>
> ˘ ´ | ´ ´ | ˘ ˘ | ˘ ´
> And brakes speed, entering the crowd.

The first line begins iambic but shifts to the trochaic for the last two feet. The line has five feet. Line 2 is totally iambic; there are four feet. Line 3 is pentameter again, five feet, a mixture of trochaic and iambic. Line 4, also pentameter, has four iambic feet and one spondaic foot. Line 5 scans as pentameter. Then lines 6 and 7 have just four poetic feet—tetrameter.

You may scan more lines, but you can determine fairly quickly that the poem is a controlled free verse rather than rhymed verse. You can also begin to see how the poet plays the trochaic beat against the iambic from time to time, as in the first line. The meter may parallel the motion of the speeding ambulance and the rhythm of the flashing red ambulance lights. Or perhaps it suggests the frantic, sometimes irregular beats of the human heart.

It is also clear that a number of lines run into one another—lines 2 and 3 and lines 4 and 5—giving the poem a continuous, connected motion.

The rhythm of the poem suggests the persona's emotional involvement in the experience. The uneven beat could show the surprise of someone who just happens upon the wreck or the horror of someone who was involved in it. Knowing who your persona is will help you decide what approach to take.

- What sound harmonies stand out in the poem?

Although there is almost no rhyme, Shapiro makes excellent use of alliteration throughout the poem: "soft silver," "bell beating, beating," "down" and "dark." There is also assonance—the *ow* in "crowd," "down," and "out;" the long *o* sound in "cargo," "doors," and "closed." Go through the poem and pick out other harmonies. Notice particularly how the *s* sound is used throughout the last stanza as a connecting link. Remember, marking the harmonies can help you use your voice to enhance the poem's meaning.

Certainly you will play with all the harmonies in some way as you read, but you may decide to focus on one particular sound or set of sounds because they relate in some specific way to your persona. For instance, if your persona is a quiet, sensitive person, you may want to concentrate on the easy *s* that runs through the poem.

- What images and figures of speech stand out in the poem?

The poem opens by suggesting sound, a "quick soft silver bell." The second and third lines appeal to sight—a "ruby flare" that pulses "red light." The red light is "like an artery," a simile. The "doors leap open" is an example of personification. Lanterns are "Empty husks of locusts," a metaphor. Throats are "tight as tourniquets," another simile. The poem literally explodes with vivid images; and once you identify them, you can respond to them and share them, vocally and physically, with your audience.

- How does the poem build?

At what point does the poem progress to its greatest revelation? What is the high point, the climax? Even though there is no plot, there is movement to a point of highest intensity, a crescendo of emotion. It is important for you to identify that point so that you, through your persona, can vocally and physically reflect the poem's movement. Probably the last lines of the third stanza represent the moment of climax in "Auto Wreck." Here the persona admits "touching a wound/That opens to our richest horror." Then, beginning with the last stanza, the poem moves toward its resolution, the speaker's coming to a painful realization.

Introducing the Interpretation

Now that you have studied the poem, you are ready to create an introduction for the selection. With all introductions, remember that you are introducing both yourself and the work of literature you will read. Be sure that your words give insight into the selection you are presenting, and, if possible, some indication as to why the literature has significance for you. You must name the selection and the author after your introduction.

One student who performed "Auto Wreck" used the following introduction.

> Two weeks ago my dad was driving me home from soccer practice when he skidded on wet pavement and slammed into a telephone pole. Luckily, neither of us was seriously hurt, but still I can hear the crunch of crumpling metal, the tinkle of broken glass. Every time I get in a car I feel a kind of tension. Karl Shapiro carries us into the terror and tension of another accident as he walks us through the scene of an "Auto Wreck."

A second approach to introducing the poem might be to focus on images, creating an atmosphere suggestive of the poem.

> Imagine a quiet, peaceful night shattered by the sound of a car skidding on pavement and then slamming into a light pole. Suddenly a multitude of sounds blend together: the shattering of glass, the crunching of metal, and the screams of people. We recognize the sounds immediately and fear their meaning. An unexpected crash has brought us face to face with our own mortality, the reality of a car accident.

Once the introduction is written and polished, memorize it so that you can speak the words in a relaxed, conversational way. Even though you may be speaking memorized words, make the delivery appear spontaneous. Talk *with,* not *at* the audience, so that the introduction invites the listeners into the experience you are about to share.

Activity 2   Preparing an Introduction

1. Examine the two introductions suggested for "Auto Wreck." What different qualities does each possess? Which introduction do you like better? Why?

2. Write an introduction for "A Lover's Toy," page 60, or "Deer Hunt," page 52. Share the introduction with fellow class members and have them evaluate what you have written. It is important that the evaluator be able to explain the reason for her or his assessment.

3. Practice saying the introduction until you can speak it from memory. Present your introduction to a partner and get feedback on the effectiveness of your delivery. ■

Exploring Options for Performance

As you prepare material for interpretation, be aware of the various possibilities for a poetry performance depending on the amount of time allowed. Popular lengths for poetry interpretations are five minutes, seven minutes, and ten minutes. Whatever the length, you will find some poems which can stand alone in filling the time. You need do nothing more than select the poem, write an introduction, rehearse, and then present it.

Some poems, however, are too long for the time allowed. If that is the case, you will need to do some excerpting or cutting to make the poem conform to established time limitations. Excerpting means taking a part of a poem which could stand alone and using it as is. Stephen Vincent Benet's epic *John Brown's Body* has a number of sections that easily can be excerpted for interpretation. Cutting a poem, on the other hand, can be difficult, particularly if there is distinctive rhyme and rhythm. In the editing process you have to be careful to preserve both the content and the rhythmic flow of the poem. As an interpreter, you are not at liberty to murder the author's metrical structure or poetic intent. So edit with integrity.

Because a majority of lyric poems are too short to fill the suggested time for an effective interpretation, it is often convenient to put together a kind of program that contains two or more poems. Numerous options are available. You may choose to interpret two or three poems on the same subject, poems that present contrasting or even complementary views. The poems may be written by the same author or different authors. Such programs are **theme-centered,** connected by subject or concept. Possible themes would include war, people at work, people at play, human qualities of animals, exploration and discovery, rebels, growing up, lost love, dieting, sports, rivers, dancing, relatives. The list could go on and on. Any theme or subject can work. What matters is that the poems have some clear connection that becomes the focus of your interpretation.

Some programs are **poet-centered:** they take a single poet and show different stages of his or her career, different insights into similar situations, various character portraits, or any of a number of other possibilities. What connects this kind of program is the writer, and the focus is on what the poet does.

As with any interpretation, there will be an introduction. The introduction should clarify the connection that ties the program together. As an interpreter, you may choose to introduce all the poems in the opening introduction or one at a time as you move through the program.

Even if you name all the poems and poets in your opening introduction, you may still need to develop transitions to connect the poems that are part of the program.

If the poems come from different periods of a poet's career, for example, you might point out something about the particular phase the poem represents, particularly showing what is unique about that phase. If you are building around a theme, you may want to point out the developmental process of that theme or different qualities of the specific theme you are exploring.

Like the introduction, the transitions should be presented from memory and spoken with naturalness, ease, and spontaneity. They should reflect the interpreter's insight and lead the audience smoothly from selection to selection.

Bringing Poetry to Life

The final step, then, is to bring the interpretation to life vocally and physically. Since most poetry interpretation is done with script in hand, you need to learn how to work from a manuscript. Generally, it is best to work from a typed copy of the selection held in a notebook. Some people like working from loose-leaf notebooks nine inches by twelve inches with three-quarter-inch rings. The most popular size folder, however, is six inches by nine inches with one-inch rings. Find the size folder that best suits you.

During the introduction, the closed notebook is held comfortably in front of the performer or at her or his side. At the conclusion of the introduction, the performer opens the folder and holds it with both hands in a position for easy reading.

During the reading, the face and body should respond to the literature. Wild movement can be obtrusive, but responsive expression and gestures that fit the persona can enhance the words and help convey precise meaning. As an interpreter, be aware of how body tension, simple hand gestures, and expressive use of the face, particularly the eyes, can reinforce the written word, helping the audience to sense what is being shared through the performance. Your job is not to act out the poem; but no interpretation seems complete without some bodily reaction to suggest the action and to clarify meaning.

The persona may either speak directly to the audience or address another person. In the latter case, you will need to establish a focal point for that unseen listener. If there are a number of characters who speak, you will need a clear focal point for each one, just as you learned while working with prose. Focal points are important in poetry, too, to help establish character placement and character relationships.

To guide you as you read, it may be helpful to mark the script, to **score** it, so as to indicate where you wish to slow down or speed up the tempo and when you wish to pause. Marking words that need special coloring, especially verbs that need emphasizing to convey action or adjectives that need shading to shape meaning, can be very helpful. Many interpreters like to develop their own system of marking, everything from using slashes—a single for a short pause and a double for a longer pause—to using a squiggly line to indicate the need for the voice to show the texture suggested in a word such as *scratchy* or *velvety*. Some interpreters use different colored markers. The best method is the one that meets your personal needs.

Activity 3   Putting It All Together

1. Following are several poems. Select one and prepare it for presentation. Study the poem carefully, write an introduction, practice your vocal and physical delivery, and then interpret the poem for an audience.

Getting Started in Oral Interpretation

"Ah, Are You Digging on My Grave?"

by Thomas Hardy

"Ah, are you digging on my grave,
    My loved one?—planting rue?"
—"No: yesterday he went to wed
One of the brightest wealth has bred.
'It cannot hurt her how,' he said,
'That I should not be true.' "

"Then who is digging on my grave?
    My nearest dearest kin?"
—"Ah, no: they sit and think, 'What use!
What good will planting flowers produce?
No tendance of her mount can loose
    Her spirit from Death's gin.' "

"But some one digs upon my grave?
    My enemy?—prodding sly?"
—"Nay: when she heard you had passed the Gate
That shuts on all flesh soon or late,
She thought you no more worth her hate,
    And cares not where you lie."

"Then, who is digging on my grave?
    Say—since I have not guessed!"
—"O it is I, my mistress dear,
Your little dog, who still lives near,
And much I hope my movements here
    Have not disturbed your rest?"

"Ah, yes! *You* dig upon my grave . . .
    Why flashed it not on me
That one true heart was left behind!
What feeling do we ever find
To equal among human kind
    A dog's fidelity!"

"Mistress, I dug upon your grave
    To bury a bone, in case
I should be hungry near this spot
When passing on my daily trot.
I am sorry, but I quite forgot
    It was your resting-place."

"Oranges"

by Gary Soto

The first time I walked
With a girl, I was twelve,
Cold, and weighted down
With two oranges in my jacket.
December. Frost cracking
Beneath my steps, my breath
Before me, then gone,

As I walked toward
Her house, the one whose
Porchlight burned yellow
Night or day, in any weather.
A dog barked at me, until
She came out pulling
At her gloves, face bright
With rouge. I smiled,
Touched her shoulder, and led
Her down the street, across
A used car lot and a line
Of newly planted trees,
Until we were breathing
Before a drug store. We
Entered, the tiny bell
Bringing a saleslady
Down a narrow aisle of goods.
I turned to the candies
Tiered like bleachers,
And asked what she wanted—
Light in her eyes, a smile
Starting at the corners
Of her mouth. I fingered
A nickel in my pocket,
And when she lifted a chocolate
That cost a dime,
I didn't say anything.
I took the nickel from
My pocket, then an orange,
And set them quietly on
The counter. When I looked up,
The lady's eyes met mine,
And held them, knowing
Very well what it was all
About.

    Outside,
A few cars hissing past,
Fog hanging like old
Coats between the trees.
I took my girl's hand
In mine for two blocks,
Then released it to let
Her unwrap the chocolate.
I peeled my orange
That was so bright against
The gray December
That, from some distance,
Someone might have thought
I was making a fire in my hands.

"The Runaway"

by Robert Frost

Once when the snow of the year was beginning to fall,
We stopped by a mountain pasture to say, "Whose colt?"
A little Morgan had one forefoot on the wall,
The other curled at his breast. He dipped his head
And snorted at us. And then he had to bolt.
We heard the miniature thunder where he fled,
And saw him, or thought we saw him, dim and grey
Like a shadow against the curtain of falling flakes.
"I think the little fellow's afraid of the snow.
He isn't winter-broken. It isn't play
With the little fellow at all. He's running away.
I doubt if even his mother could tell him, 'Sakes,
It's only weather.' He'd think she didn't know!
Where is his mother? He can't be out alone."
And now he comes again with clatter of stone,
And mounts the wall again with whited eyes
And all his tail that isn't hair up straight.
He shudders his coat as if to throw off flies.
"Whoever it is that leaves him out so late,
When other creatures have gone to stall and bin,
Ought to be told to come and take him in."

"PORPHYRIA'S LOVER"

by Robert Browning

The rain set early in to-night,
   The sullen wind was soon awake,
It tore the elm-tops down for spite,
   And did its worst to vex the lake:
I listened with heart fit to break.
When glided in Porphyria; straight
   She shut the cold out and the storm,
And kneeled and made the cheerless grate
   Blaze up, and all the cottage warm;
Which done, she rose, and from her form
Withdrew the dripping cloak and shawl,
   And laid her soiled gloves by, untied
Her hat and let the damp hair fall,
   And last, she sat down by my side
And called me. When no voice replied,
She put my arm about her waist,
   And made her smooth white shoulder bare
And all her yellow hair displaced,
   And, stooping, made my cheek lie there,
And spread, o'er all, her yellow hair,
Murmuring how she loved me—she
   Too weak, for all her heart's endeavor,
To set its struggling passion free
   From pride, and vainer ties dissever,
And give herself to me forever.
But passion sometimes would prevail,
   Nor could to-night's gay feast restrain
A sudden thought of one so pale
   For love of her, and all in vain:
So, she was come through wind and rain,
Be sure I looked up at her eyes
   Happy and proud; at last I knew
Porphyria worshiped me; surprise
   Made my heart swell, and still it grew
While I debated what to do.
That moment she was mine, mine, fair,
   Perfectly pure and good: I found

A thing to do, and all her hair
    In one long yellow string I wound
Three times her little throat around,
And strangled her. No pain felt she;
    I am quite sure she felt no pain.
As a shut bud that holds a bee,
    I warily oped her lids: again
Laughed the blue eyes without a stain.
And I untightened next the tress
    About her neck; her cheek once more
Blushed bright beneath my burning kiss:
    I propped her head up as before,
Only, this time my shoulder bore
Her head, which droops upon it still:
    The smiling rosy little head,
So glad it has its utmost will,
    That all it scorned at once is fled,
And I, its love, am gained instead!
Porphyria's love: she guessed now how
    Her darling one which would be heard,
And thus we sit together now,
    And all night long we have not stirred,
And yet God has not said a word!

"MY MOTHER PIECED QUILTS"

by Teresa Palomo Acosta

They were just meant as covers
in winter
as weapons
against pounding january winds

but it was just that every morning I awoke to these
october ripened canvases
passed my hand across their cloth faces
and began to wonder how you pieced
all these together
these strips of gentle communion cotton and
    flannel nightgowns
wedding organdies
dime store velvets

how you shaped patterns square and oblong and
    round
positioned
balanced
then cemented them
with your thread
a steel needle
a thimble

how the thread darted in and out
galloping along the frayed edges, tucking them in
as you did us at night

oh how you stretched and turned and re-arranged
your michigan spring faded curtain pieces
my father's santa fe work shirt
the sunnier denims, the tweeds of fall

in the evening you sat at your canvas
—our cracked linoleum floor the drawing board
me lounging on your arm
and you staking out the plan:
whether to put the lilac purple of easter against the
    red plaid of winter-going
into-spring
whether to mix a yellow with blue and white and
    paint the
corpus christi noon when my father held your
    hand
whether to shape a five-point star from the
somber black silk you wore to grandmother's
    funeral

you were the river current
carrying the roaring notes
forming them into pictures of a little boy reclining
a swallow flying
you were the caravan master at the reins
driving your threaded needle artillery across the
    mosaic cloth bridges
delivering yourself in separate testimonies.

oh mother you plunged me sobbing and laughing
into our past
into the river crossing at five
into the spinach fields
into the plainview cotton rows
into the tuberculosis wards
into braids and muslin dresses
sewn hard and taut to withstand the thrashings of
    twenty-five years

stretched out they lay
armed/ready/shouting/celebrating

knotted with love
the quilts sing on

"Jade Flower Palace" by Tu Fu

translated from the Chinese by Kenneth Rexroth

The stream swirls. The wind moans in
The pines. Gray rats scurry over
Broken tiles. What price, long ago,
Built this palace, standing in
Ruins beside the cliffs? There are
Green ghost fires in the black rooms.

Getting Started in Oral Interpretation

The shattered pavements are
All washed away. Ten thousand organ
Pipes whistle and roar. The storm
Scatters the red autumn leaves.
His dancing girls are yellow dust.
Their painted cheeks have crumbled
Away. His gold chariots
And courtiers are gone. Only
A stone horse is left of his
Glory. I sit on the grass and
Start a poem, but the pathos of
It overcomes me. The future
Slips imperceptibly away.
Who can say what the years will bring?

2. Make your own selection of a poem or poems for interpretation. Work within a minimum time of three minutes and a maximum time limit of seven minutes, including intro- duction and transitions, if there are any. You may choose to prepare a single poem, or you may decide to put together a program. Go through all parts of the preparation process as you analyze, practice, and prepare for performance. Then present your interpretation for an audience. ■

7 Analyzing Drama

Matching Wits with the Best . . .

Imagine yourself as a brilliant detective, known throughout the world for your ability to ferret out the most minute clues, put them together logically, and construct a scenario which solves crimes that other super sleuths find baffling. Surely such work could be challenging, exciting, and rewarding.

As an interpreter of drama, you need to be just this type of clever inspector—a literary detective. You must dig out the facts and clues concealed in a play, draw logical conclusions from the play's hints and implications, and construct complex characters whom you will bring to life for your audience.

Dramatic literature is different from prose fiction and poetry in that it does not feature a narrator who relates the events of the story or a person who speaks the words of a poem. Instead, dramatic literature consists entirely of the characters speaking directly to each other.* In the absence of the narrator, the playwright conveys the information about characters mainly in the spoken lines of the play. So that such information is not awkwardly obvious to the playgoers, the author presents it with great subtlety. The playwright does not deliberately *hide* the information but rather presents it indirectly. As a literary detective, you must gather these half-concealed clues and employ them to portray the complex characters the author has created.

How should you begin your detective work? As suggested in Chapter 1, whenever possible you should start with a reading of the entire play from which your selection or excerpt comes. Get an intuitive sense of the full play and the characters before you start a more systematic exploration. When you feel you have such a good general understanding, you are ready to put on your double-billed cap, take out your magnifying glass, and go hunting for those elusive clues.

---

* Some modern plays do feature a narrator who tells some of the story, *Our Town* by Thornton Wilder and *The Glass Menagerie* by Tennessee Williams, for example; but in each instance, most of the play consists of characters relating directly to each other.

Sensing the Structure

You probably know that most plays, like most novels, short stories, and narrative poems, follow a multi-part structure. Initially you encounter the **exposition,** where the author presents the characters and the situation; next there's the **inciting incident,** which sets the plot into motion; after that come the **rising action,** where the "plot thickens"; the **crisis,** the turning point after which only one outcome is possible; and the **climax,** the high point to which everything has been building. Then finally there's the **denouement,** the resolution of all matters. This pattern has been compared to the ill-fated flight of an airplane: The exposition is the plane starting down the runway; the inciting incident is a serious but undetected puncture of the fuel tank; the rising action includes the takeoff, the crew's discovery of the leak, and their unsuccessful attempts to find a landing place; the crisis occurs the moment the plane runs out of fuel; the climax is the crash; and the denouement is the cleanup of the wreckage!

Concentrating on Conflict

While it is important to understand how the play is structured, your major concern in the interpretation of drama is the creation of believable characters in conflict. In this respect, drama is like a game with the main character or **protagonist** fighting to win over his or her opponent, the **antagonist.** In each scene you perform, you will need to locate the conflict as it creates the tension that drives the scene forward and holds the audience's interest. Every scene should focus on some conflict between the characters in it. That's what makes drama exciting: Each character is determined to win the encounter. The stakes may be low, such as deciding who should do the dishes, or very high, such as deciding the victor of a life-and-death battle. The higher the stakes, the more gripping the encounter will be.

Any scene you perform will start with characters attempting to achieve conflicting goals, and it will end when one of the characters succeeds and the other fails in his or her efforts. Thus every scene you perform in a way mirrors the structure of the whole play, beginning with a conflict that builds to a climax and ending with some kind of resolution. At the start of your preparation, find the conflicts in the scene, for they will be the heart of your performance.

Of course conflict depends on contrasting characters, and as an interpreter of drama you must be especially skilled in creating believable human beings. Even if you are performing a broadly comic scene, you need to keep the characters realistic. Though their actions may be extreme, the characters must not be pushed over the line into **caricature** or they will not be genuinely funny.

Good playwrights tend to create characters that are richly detailed or **rounded;** those who are less complex are called **flat characters.** Usually the best performances result from portrayals of rounded characters totally fleshed out. For this reason, you want to learn as much as possible about the characters you will embody. As a literary detective, you may undertake a number of investigations to help you find the information you need.

One aspect you want to investigate is the characters' intentions in the scene you perform. Be sure you know what each character is trying to achieve in your scene. Some performers ask themselves, "What is each character *fighting* to gain?" If a character's intention in a scene is not clear to you, you may want to think in terms of what the character is trying to achieve in the whole play. Knowing the answer to that question can often lead you to an answer about his or her intentions in a scene, as a character tends to fight for specific minor goals that will lead her or him to the major goal, just as a mason lays individual bricks in order to achieve the objective of building a wall. Ask yourself, in addition, what the character is attempting to achieve in every line so that you can focus moment by moment on what he or she is struggling to accomplish.

A Play to Probe

Carefully read the following short play, "A Defenseless Creature." It is part of Neil Simon's comedy *The Good Doctor,* a play based on the works of Anton Chekhov, the great Russian writer of plays and short stories. The script will tell you what you need to know to complete a number of activities in this chapter. As you will probably surmise, the play is set in Russia during the late 1800s.

"A DEFENSELESS CREATURE"

The lights come up on the office of a bank official, Kistunov. *He enters on a crutch; his right foot is heavily encased in bandages, swelling it to three times its normal size. He suffers from the gout and is very careful of any mishap which would only intensify his pain. He makes it to his desk and sits. An* Assistant, *rather harried, enters.*

Assistant:	*(With volume)* Good morning, Mr. Kistunov!
Kistunov:	Shhh! Please . . . Please lower your voice.
Assistant:	*(Whispers)* I'm sorry, sir.
Kistunov:	It's just that my gout is acting up again and my nerves are like little firecrackers. The least little friction can set them off.
Assistant:	It must be *very* painful, sir.
Kistunov:	Combing my hair this morning was agony.
Assistant:	Mr. Kistunov . . .
Kistunov:	What is it, Pochatkin?
Assistant:	There's a woman who insists on seeing you. We can't make head or tail out of her story, but she insists on seeing the directing manager. Perhaps if you're not well—
Kistunov:	No, no. The business of the bank comes before my minor physical ailments. Show her in, please . . . quietly. *(The* Assistant *tiptoes out. A* Woman *enters. She is in her late forties, poorly dressed. She is of the working class. She crosses to the desk, a forlorn look on her face. She twists her bag nervously.)* Good morning, madame. Forgive me for not standing, but I am somewhat incapacitated. Please sit down.
Woman:	Thank you. *(She sits.)*
Kistunov:	Now, what can I do for you?
Woman:	You can help me, sir. I pray to God you can help. No one else in this world seems to care . . . *(And she begins to cry, which in turn becomes a wail—the kind of wail that melts the spine of strong men.* Kistunov *winces and grits his teeth in pain as he grips the arms of his chair.)*
Kistunov:	Calm yourself, madame. I *beg* of you. Please calm yourself.
Woman:	I'm sorry. *(She tries to calm down.)*
Kistunov:	I'm sure we can sort it all out if we approach the problem sensibly and quietly . . . Now, what exactly is your trouble?
Woman:	Well, sir . . . It's my husband. Collegiate Assessor Schukin. He's been sick for five months . . . Five agonizing months.

Kistunov:	(Delicately) I know the horrors of illness and can sympathize with you, madame. What's the nature of his illness?
Woman:	It's a nervous disorder. Everything grates on his nerves. If you so much as touch him he'll scream out—(And without warning, she screams a loud bloodcurdling scream that sends Kistunov almost out of his seat.) How or why he got it, nobody knows.
Kistunov:	(Trying to regain his composure) I have an inkling . . . Please go on, a little less descriptively, if possible.
Woman:	Well, while the poor man was lying in bed—
Kistunov:	(Braces himself) You're not going to scream again, are you?
Woman:	Not that I don't have cause . . . While he was lying in bed these five months, recuperating, he was dismissed from his job—for no reason at all.
Kistunov:	That's a pity, certainly, but I don't quite see the connection with our bank, madame.
Woman:	You don't know how I suffered during his illness. I nursed him from morning till night. Doctored him from night till morning. Besides cleaning my house, taking care of my children, feeding our dog, our cat, our goat, my sister's bird, who was sick . . .
Kistunov:	The bird was sick?
Woman:	My sister! She gets dizzy spells. She's been dizzy a month now. And she's getting dizzier every day . . .
Kistunov:	Extraordinary. However—
Woman:	I had to take care of her children and her house and her cat and her goat, and then her bird bit one of my children, and our cat bit her bird, so my oldest daughter, the one with the broken arm, drowned my sister's cat, and now my sister wants my goat in exchange, or else she says she'll either drown my cat or break my oldest daughter's other arm—
Kistunov:	Yes, well, you've certainly had your pack of troubles, haven't you? But I don't quite see—
Woman:	And then, when I went to get my husband's pay, they deducted twenty-four rubles and thirty-six kopecks. For what? I asked. Because, they said, he borrowed it from the employees' fund. But that's impossible. He could never borrow without my approval. I'd break his arm . . . Not while he was sick, of course . . . I don't have the strength. I'm not well myself, sir. I have this racking cough that's a terrible thing to hear—(She coughs rackingly—so rackingly that Kistunov is about to crack.)
Kistunov:	I can well understand why your husband took five months to recuperate . . . But what is it that you want from me, madame?
Woman:	What rightfully belongs to my husband—his twenty-four rubles and thirty-six kopecks. They won't give it to me because I'm a woman, weak and defenseless. Some of them have laughed in my face, sir . . . Laughed! (She laughs loud and painfully. Kistunov clenches everything.) Where's the humor, I wonder, in a poor, defenseless creature like myself? (She sobs.)
Kistunov:	None . . . I see none at all. However, madame, I don't wish to be unkind, but I'm afraid you've come to the wrong place. Your petition, no matter how justified, has nothing to do with us. You'll have to go to the agency where your husband was employed.
Woman:	What do you mean? I've been to five agencies already and none of them will even listen to my petition. I'm about to lose my mind. The hair is

coming out of my head. *(She pulls out a handful)* Look at my hair. By the fistful. *(She throws a fistful on his desk.)* Don't tell me to go to another agency!

Kistunov: *(Delicately and disgustedly, he picks up her fistful of hair and hands it back to her. She sticks it back in her hair.)* Please, madame, keep your hair in its proper place. Now listen to me carefully. This-is-a-bank. A bank! We're in the banking business. We bank money. Funds that are brought here are banked by us. Do you understand what I'm saying?

Woman: What are you saying?

Kistunov: I'm saying that I can't help you.

Woman: Are you saying you can't help me?

Kistunov: *(Sighs deeply)* I'm trying. I don't think I'm making headway.

Woman: Are you saying you won't believe my husband is sick? Here! Here is a doctor's certificate *(She puts it on the desk and pounds it.)* There's the proof. Do you still doubt that my husband is suffering from a nervous disorder?

Kistunov: Not only do I not doubt it, I would *swear* to it.

Woman: *Look at it! You didn't look at it!*

Kistunov: It's really not necessary. I know *full well* how your husband must be suffering.

Woman: *What's the point in a doctor's certificate if you don't look at it?!* LOOK AT IT!

Kistunov: *(Frightened, quickly looks at it.)* Oh, yes . . . I see your husband is sick. It's right here on the doctor's certificate. Well, you certainly have a good case, madame, but I'm afraid you've *still come to the wrong place. (Getting perplexed)* I'm getting excited.

Woman: *(Stares at him)* You lied to me. I took you as a man of your word and you lied to me.

Kistunov: I? LIE? WHEN?

Woman: *(Snatches the certificate)* When you said you read the doctor's certificate. You couldn't have. You couldn't have read the description of my husband's illness without seeing he was fired unjustly. *(She puts the certificate back on the desk.)* Don't take advantage of me just because I'm a weak, defenseless woman. Do me the simple courtesy of reading the doctor's certificate. That's all I ask. Read it, and then I'll go.

Kistunov: But I *read it!* What's the point in reading something twice when I've already *read it once?*

Woman: You didn't read it carefully.

Kistunov: I read it *in detail!*

Woman: Then you read it too fast. Read it slower.

Kistunov: *I don't have to read it slower. I'm a fast reader.*

Woman: Maybe you didn't absorb it. Let it sink in this time.

Kistunov: *(Almost apoplectic)* I *absorbed* it! It *sank* in! I could pass a *test* on what's written here, *but it doesn't make any difference because it has nothing to do with our bank!*

Woman: *(She throws herself on him from behind.)* Did you read the part where it says he has a nervous disorder? Read that part again and see if I'm wrong.

Kistunov:	THAT PART? OH, YES! I SEE YOUR HUSBAND HAS A NERVOUS DISORDER. MY, MY, HOW TERRIBLE! ONLY I CAN'T HELP YOU! NOW PLEASE GO! *(He falls back into his chair, exhausted.)*
Woman:	*(Crosses to where his foot is resting)* I'm sorry, Excellency. I hope I haven't caused you any pain.
Kistunov:	*(Trying to stop her)* Please, don't kiss my foot. *(He is too late—she has given his foot a most ardent embrace. He screams in pain.)* Agggghhh! Can't you get this into your balding head? If you would just realize that to come to us with this kind of claim is as strange as your trying to get a haircut from a butcher shop.
Woman:	You can't get a haircut in a butcher shop. Why would anyone go to a butcher shop for a haircut? Are you laughing at me?
Kistunov:	*Laughing!* I'm lucky I'm breathing . . . Pochatkin!
Woman:	Did I tell you I'm fasting? I haven't eaten in three days. I want to eat, but nothing stays down. I had the same cup of coffee three times today.
Kistunov:	*(With his last burst of energy, screams)* POCHATKIN!
Woman:	I'm skin and bones. I faint at the least provocation . . . Watch. *(She swoons to the floor.)* Did you see? You saw how I just fainted? Eight times a day that happens.
	(The assistant rushes in.)
Assistant:	What is it, Mr. Kistunov? What's wrong?
Kistunov:	*(Screams)* GET HER OUT OF HERE! Who let her in my office?
Assistant:	You did, sir. I asked you and you said, "Show her in."
Kistunov:	I thought you meant a human being, not a lunatic with a doctor's certificate.
Woman:	*(To Pochatkin)* He wouldn't even read it. I gave it to him, he threw it back in my face . . . You look like a kind person. Have pity on me. *You* read it and see if my husband is sick or not.
	(She forces the certificate on Pochatkin.)
Assistant:	I *read* it, madame. Twice!
Kistunov:	Me too. I had to read it twice too.
Assistant:	You just showed it to me outside. You showed it to to *everyone*. We *all* read it. Even the doorman.
Woman:	You just looked at it. You didn't read it.
Kistunov:	Don't argue. Read it, Pochatkin. For God's sake, read it so we can get her out of here.
Assistant:	*(Quickly scans it)* Oh, yes. It says your husband is sick. *(He looks up; gives it back to her.)* Now will you please leave, madame, or I will have to get someone to remove you.
Kistunov:	Yes! Yes! Good! Remove her! Get the doorman and two of the guards. Be careful, she's strong as an ox.
Woman:	*(To Kistunov)* If you touch me, I'll scream so loud they'll hear me all over the city. You'll lose all your depositors. No one will come to a bank where they beat weak, defenseless women . . . I think I'm going to faint again . . . .
Kistunov:	*(Rising)* WEAK? DEFENSELESS? You are as defenseless as a charging rhinoceros! You are as weak as the King of the Jungle! You are a plague,

madame! A plague that wipes out all that crosses your path! You are a raging river that washes out bridges and stately homes! You are a wind that blows villages over mountains! It is women like you who drive men like me to the condition of husbands like yours!

Woman: Are you saying you are not going to help me?

Kistunov: Hit her, Pochatkin! Strike her! I give you permission to knock her down. Beat some sense into her!

Woman: *(To Pochatkin)* You hear? You hear how I'm abused? He would have you hit an orphaned mother. Did you hear me cough? Listen to this cough. *(She "racks" up another coughing spell.)*

Assistant: Madame, if we can discuss this in my office— *(He takes her arm.)*

Woman: Get your hands off me . . . Help! Help! I'm being beaten! Oh merciful God, they're beating me!

Assistant: I am not beating you. I am just holding your arm.

Kistunov: Beat her, you fool. Kick her while you've got the chance. We'll never get her out of here. Knock her senseless! *(He tries to kick her, misses and falls to the floor).*

Woman: *(Pointing an evil finger at Kistunov, she jumps on the desk and punctuates each sentence by stepping on his desk bell.)* A curse! A curse on your bank! I put a curse on you and your depositors! May the money in your vaults turn to potatoes! May the gold in your cellars turn to onions! May your rubles turn to radishes, and your kopecks to pickles . . .

Kistunov: STOP! Stop it, I beg of you! . . . Pochatkin, give her the money. Give her what she wants. Give her anything—only get her out of here!

Woman: *(To Pochatkin)* Twenty-four rubles and thirty-six kopecks . . . Not a penny more. That's all that's due to me and that's all I want.

Assistant: Come with me, I'll get you the money.

Woman: And another ruble to get me home. I'd walk but I have very weak ankles.

Kistunov: Give her enough for a taxi, anything, only get her out.

Woman: God bless you, sir. You're a kind man. I remove the curse. *(With a gesture)* Curse be gone! Onions to money, potatoes to gold—

Kistunov: *(Pulls on his hair)* REMOVE HERRRR! Oh, God, my hair is falling out! *(He pulls some hair out.)*

Woman: Oh, there's one other thing, sir. I'll need a letter of recommendation so my husband can get another job. Don't bother about it today. I'll be back in the morning. God bless you, sir . . . *(She leaves.)*

Kistunov: She's coming back . . . She's coming back . . . *(He slowly begins to go mad and takes his cane and begins to beat his bandaged leg.)* She's coming back . . . She's coming back . . .

(Dim-out)

Activity 1 Identifying Conflicting Intentions

1. What is the woman's main intention in coming to the bank?
2. What does she specifically want from Kistunov? List at least five things that she tries to get him to do.
3. What is Kistunov's main intention in the scene?
4. What actions does he do to accomplish that intention?
5. What specific strategies does he use to try to counter her demands? List at least five actions he does to oppose this "defenseless" woman. ■

Combing the Content

An effective way for you to investigate characters in a play is to go over the text with a fine-tooth comb. In other words, you go through a script and write down every detail about the character. If you do an excerpt from a long play—and usually that is what you will do—it is essential to comb the *entire* play, for the playwright will provide important clues for characterization throughout the script. The combing process may be somewhat time-consuming, but the rewards it pays in enabling you to build rich characterizations are worth the effort.

Here is a sample combing of the first part of "A Defenseless Creature." Notice how the details are provided in two columns with the information appearing in the order that it appears in the play.

Kistunov	Woman (Mrs. Schukin)
name suggests Russian nationality	in late 40s
bank official (directing manager)	poorly dressed
uses crutch	belongs to working class
right foot is swollen and bandaged	habitually twists handbag
has gout	cries or wails easily
wants absolute quiet	husband is Collegiate Assessor Schukin
nerves are "like little firecrackers"	husband has been ill five months with a nervous disorder
sensitive to pain	screams to demonstrate husband's agony
says combing his hair was agony	husband has lost his job
puts bank business ahead of his own problems	says she's nursed husband night and day during his illness
insists on quiet	has had difficult life caring for her family and animals
grits his teeth to bear pain	has sister with dizzy spells
is initially very courteous to woman	has had to take care of sister's duties
logical	her family and animals fight with her sister's family and animals
feels bank has no responsibility to help her	wants 24 rubles and 36 kopecks
understands that wife's abrasive personality contributed to her husband's illness	says she would have broken husband's arm for borrowing without her approval
nearly cracks from hearing woman's cough	says she wouldn't break his arm when he's sick
	claims to be ill with racking cough

1. Using the sample given to get you started, complete the combing of "A Defenseless Creature." Use the double-column format used in the sample. Read carefully so that you capture not only the facts the author presents about the characters but also the conclusions you can draw about them.

2. Using the information you have discovered through your combing, translate the major traits into possible physical actions you think help embody them. You might think of people you know to use as examples.

3. Now with a partner or a small group, discuss key options for characterization you have devised as a result of your individual study. ■

Succeeding with the Subtext

Another valuable tool to help you prepare a richly detailed performance is a **subtext,** which is an indication of what is happening under the lines of the script. In real life a great deal is constantly occurring in your mind and body that no one but you is aware of. And yet those thoughts and feelings do influence your moods, your speech, and your actions. The purpose of the subtext is to help you consider those same processes as they affect the characters you portray.

A subtext has a number of different aspects. The first is the character's *thoughts*. You know that you don't say everything that pops into your mind. In fact, you couldn't if you tried, for your brain works much faster than your mouth! But more importantly, the things you *don't* say may be a better indication of your real feelings than what you *do* say. Often what people say is the opposite of what they really think. For example, you may smile at a friend and say, "Sure, it'd be great to go to your little sister's piano recital with you," when you're really thinking, "I'd rather have my teeth pulled than sit through two hours of tinkling torment." In the play *Dino* by Reginald Rose, a caseworker asks the angry Dino, "Did something happen last night, Dino?" The unhappy young man snaps back, "No!" He really means, "Yes!" When a character says one thing while thinking the opposite, there emerges a complexity of meaning that makes the character more rounded than flat and hence much more interesting to an audience.

Another part of the subtext is the character's *memories*. In real life, the activities you do often remind you of past events, if only for a moment. In fact, your mind is bombarded with mental pictures of events from the past, almost as if snapshots were flashing in your head. These pictures change so swiftly that you probably can't recall a sustained action; thus they seem more like slide shows than like movies in your mind. When your friend asked you to attend the piano recital, an image of a black baby grand piano may have flashed into your mind, followed by an image of a six-year-old girl in a frilly, white dress. When Dino says, "No!" in answer to the caseworker's question, a picture of his father's face, distorted in anger, may flash in his mind, for the event that he's trying to avoid discussing is a terrible encounter with his father that happened the previous night. If you as a performer can let your mind conjure up the image that might occur in the character's mind, you will be able to connect with the character more richly than you would without these images. Thus your character will have more depth and be more convincing to your audience than the characters of performers who haven't considered such matters.

The third part of subtext is the character's *sensations,* anything that the character sees, hears, smells, tastes, or feels. As a living creature, you are constantly receiving messages from the world around you. If you pause for a moment to notice what's happening around you, you'll probably be surprised at all your body is experiencing. What sounds do you hear—the rustling of papers? the buzzing of fluorescent lights? the passing of cars outside? What do your eyes pick out as you gaze around the room—a classmate's new watch? a colorful poster on the wall? a student passing the doorway? What can you taste—perhaps some gum in your mouth? What do you smell—maybe someone's cologne? What do you feel—the temperature of the room? your back against the desk? a pang of hunger in your stomach? If you can imagine such sensations for the characters you portray, you will create an environment for the scene that will help you to feel as if you are right where the characters are. Think how the sound track of a movie helps you feel a part of the scene. Through imagining similar tracks for all five senses, you can do a great deal to make the scene real for you, your characters, and your audience.

You may wonder where these thoughts, memories, and sensations come from. The answer is that most of them are created by the interpreter but built from what the playwright has given. For example, you know from reading "A Defenseless Creature" that Kistunov is experiencing great pain. Imagine how his leg feels. Is the pain sharp or dull? steady or throbbing? extending through the whole leg or affecting just a part of it? The woman speaks of her husband. She no doubt has a mental image or memory of him. What does he look like? Is he old or young? skinny or plump? bearded or clean-shaven? The script gives you some information about his health, his job, and his domination by his wife; but within these limits you are free to imagine his looks any way you choose. The important thing is that you *do* choose specific characteristics to make him real for you.

A sample subtext for a few lines appears on page 85. Notice that it is specific in detail. Because of such detail, making a subtext is a time-consuming project; but it is worth the effort. Once you discover what's happening under and between the lines, your characterizations will become complex and lifelike.

Activity 3   Writing Subtext

1. Following the format on page 85, create a detailed subtext for a two-minute segment of "A Defenseless Creature" or a scene that you would like to perform. Use a pencil so that you can easily revise as you gain further insights about the characters. Remember that the *thoughts* column contains the *words* the speaker is thinking, words that may be the opposite of what he or she is saying aloud. The *memories* column contains the *frozen pictures* that flash into the character's mind; they record specific past moments and do not show continuing action. The *sensation* column contains those *sensory impressions* that the character experiences at that moment, what he or she may be hearing, seeing, tasting, smelling, or feeling. When you discuss what you feel, do *not* record emotions such as fear, anger, or sadness, for they are not sensations. Instead, record the physical sensations you have when you feel such emotions as fear, anger, or sadness. For instance, if you are afraid, one sensation may be that your stomach is tight; if you are angry, you may feel a throbbing in your head; and if you are sad, you may feel you have no energy.

2. Share your subtext with a partner to get feedback on how effectively you have gotten between the lines. ■

Regarding Relationships

An important part of analyzing a scene is exploring the relationships of the characters. Sometimes the characters in a play have known each other for a long time: they have an extensive past association that the playwright may or may not describe in detail. Other times, as in "A Defenseless Creature," the characters meet for the first time in the scene you perform. Although their relationship has not had time to develop extensively, they still have attitudes and reactions to one another. Also, characters have relationships with people and objects that they talk about but that do not appear on stage. For example, "defenseless" Mrs. Schukin speaks about her husband at length and mentions other relatives such as her sister and daughter. If you were preparing an interpretation of this selection, you would want to imagine how this woman relates to these people so that you could speak of them with a definite attitude when saying Mrs. Schukin's lines. Don't ever underestimate the significance of relationships; and don't be afraid to fill in missing but appropriate details to help you have a clear picture to guide you in your interpretation. Sometimes it is enough merely to examine the relationships mentally. More often, however, it is necessary to record your impressions.

Activity 4   Exploring Relationships

1. Write a paragraph of about 100 to 150 words in which you explore Kistunov's feelings about the woman or her feelings about him. Use first-person narrative so that you are writing as the character. For example, for Kistunov, you might begin something like this: "Despite an attack of gout, I dragged myself to work this morning only to be accosted by this overbearing woman with a voice like a screaming banshee." Or for the woman, you might begin like this: "Today I went to a bank hoping to collect money that was due my poor, sick husband only to come face-to-face with an insensitive oaf, an absolute monster." Use the information given in the script as the basis for your paragraph, but enrich the material with details of your own imagination. Be careful not to add any details that contradict the facts and hints provided in the script.

Text	Thought Subtext	Memory Subtext	Sensation Subtext
Kistunov: Please, madame, keep your hair in its proper place. Now listen to me carefully. This-is-a-bank. A bank! We're in the banking business. We bank money. Funds that are brought here are banked by us. Do you understand what I'm saying?	Oh no! I think I'm going to vomit. She has just pulled a whole wad of hair from her head. I've got to keep calm. I'm going to have to explain to this insane witch what a bank is. O.K., she's listening. So far, so good. She's nodding. She seems to understand. Whoops! Now she's looking puzzled. Have I made her understand at all?	The intelligent face of my two-year-old grandson Misha as he tried to understand my explanation of banking to him	Feeling stomach churning; feeling tight throat; seeing wad of gray and brown hair; feeling greasy hair between my thumb and finger; burning sensation in throat; seeing her wrinkled face and bald spot on her head; seeing her nod; seeing her get puzzled look on her face
Woman: What are you saying?	What's all this gobbledy-gook? I don't know what he's talking about. I'm afraid he's going to turn me down.	The bearded face and cold eyes of the last official who turned me down	Seeing him leaning forward with hands folded in front of him; smelling liniment from his leg
Kistunov: I'm saying that I can't help you.	I can't be polite any longer. I've just go to lay it on the line. This bank is not involved.	The nice big tub of warm water I sat in this morning	Feeling heart pounding; smelling her bad breath; seeing her face with wide-open eyes and open mouth
Woman: Are you saying you can't help me?	Did he say what I think he said? The brute! Another rejection! I can't believe it!	The face of Pochatkin as he tried to stop me from coming in here	Seeing his pursed lips; hearing the clock strike nine; tasting the garlic I burped up from breakfast
Kistunov: I'm trying. I don't think I'm making much headway.	Dear God, please let her leave. I'm at my wit's end. What more can I do to get through to this idiot? Just leave me alone—please!	The easy chair at home where I sit in the evening; the glowing fireplace in my parlor	Feeling right temple throb with sharp pain; feeling perspiration on forehead and palms
Woman: Are you saying you don't believe my husband is sick? Here! Here is a doctor's certificate. There's the proof. Do you still doubt that my husband is suffering from a nervous disorder?	I can't believe he doubts my word. He's a monster! I can prove my husband is sick. This certificate will show I'm right. Oh, he makes me so mad, but I'll show him! This will make him change his mind.	Thin, pale, open-mouthed face of my husband as I left him sleeping this morning; face of the young, kind Dr. Gudunov who gave me the certificate	Feeling crumpled papers in purse; feeling my fist hit the table; smelling salami from sandwich in my purse; seeing the wrinkled doctor's certificate on the table; seeing Kistunov's face with eyes wide open

2. Share your paragraph with a partner or with a group. Read your words in such a way as to suggest the character who is speaking and that character's attitude toward and relationship with the person being spoken about. ■

Acting and Interpretation

At this point you may be asking if all this analysis isn't more appropriate for an actor than for an interpreter. The truth is that both the actor and the interpreter need to understand in depth the characters they perform. In fact, the interpreter has a greater obligation for he or she often presents several characters whereas the actor typically portrays only one.

Then how *do* you distinguish between actors and interpreters of drama? Both the actor and the interpreter study their characters in great detail, both employ gestures, and the interpreter responds as fully as the actor to the characters being portrayed. In other words, interpretation is more than toned-down acting! Despite the similarities between the two kinds of performers, however, there are significant differences: the actor almost always memorizes her or his lines, whereas the individual interpreter of drama sometimes memorizes the scene and sometimes works from a script. In addition, actors usually employ costumes, makeup, properties, and scenery to create an illusion of reality while interpreters rarely, if ever, employ such physical aids. Most importantly, actors face each other and move about on a stage before an audience from which they are usually separated by an imaginary "fourth wall." Their focus is **onstage** as they react to other characters face-to-face. The individual interpreter, on the other hand, faces her or his audience and projects the scene and listening characters out front into the audience in what is called **offstage focus.** By doing so, the interpreter places the audience in the middle of the encounter between the speaking character in front of them and the addressed or listening character behind them. From this vantage point the audience feels caught up in the action and hence very much involved in the scene. Yet because the scene is offstage, the interpreter of drama does not move around as the actor does, and he or she is more cautious about the use of broad gestures and other movements. The movement appropriate to the interpreter of drama will be discussed in more detail in the next chapter.

8 Drama, from Printed Page to Performance

Think Back in Time . . .

Can you remember a past Halloween when you spent an exciting evening trick-or-treating? You probably put on a frightening costume; maybe you included a wig, a mask, or makeup to enhance your ghastly image. Perhaps you carried an object or prop such as a broom, sword, or jack-o-lantern to complete the effect. You were creating an image by putting on all the external aspects of a characterization. As an interpreter of drama, you will approach a characterization from the opposite direction. Instead of using costumes, makeup, and properties to create the externals of a character, you will focus more on the internals, on yourself.

Now that you have learned to make careful intellectual analyses of scripts, it is time to turn your attention to the process of translating your intellectual *understanding* into physical *innerstanding*.

Getting Physical

As was mentioned earlier, drama emphasizes realistic characters in conflict. Thus you need to pay particular attention to embodying the persons you portray. Initially, understand that you should embody the characters from head to toe. In real life, your entire body responds to electric moments—the winning touchdown scored in the last seconds of play, seeing your name on the cast list for a play. In interpretation your body must respond the same way. An appropriate short poem sums up the point:

> I had a little dog named Rover;
> And when he died, he died all over.

Whether you portray life or death, as a good interpreter you need to do it "all over."

That fact, however, does not mean that you are free to do any movement you like. In the last chapter you learned that certain movements appropriate on the stage would be inappropriate in an interpreter's performance. For example, if an actor were playing Kistunov in a stage production of "A Defenseless Creature," he would probably sit at his desk with his bandaged foot elevated on a stool. The interpreter playing Kistunov would certainly not balance on one leg with the other leg extended and crouch down as if he were sitting in a chair. The pose would be both awkward and ridiculous. Instead, the interpreter, relying on suggestion and muscle memory, stands in a certain way to suggest Kistunov has a painful foot.

Your teacher will provide the guidelines for the amount and kind of movement allowed in your assigned readings. If you should enter contests in interpretation, be certain you know the rules about movement as these rules often vary from area to area. Usually, though, excessive moving about in the performing area is inappropriate as that would suggest the action of the scene is happening on a stage in front of an audience rather than offstage in the realm of the audience. Controlled, limited movement in an area about three feet square is a good rule of thumb unless specific rules indicate otherwise.

Earlier chapters have discussed the fundamental ways you can build physical characterizations, and you may wish to review those sections before moving on. Now it's time to discuss more specific aspects you will need to know as you round out characters for the interpretation of drama. The most important thing to remember is that you want to present for your audience believable characters in conflict.

As you work to develop detailed characterizations, you need to think about what part specific movements of the body can play in creating the desired image. Such movements include gestures, mannerisms, and pantomime.

Gesture is the general term used to refer to any movement of the body that conveys an idea, whether that movement is a change in body tension, an adjustment in posture, or some specific movement of the hands and arms.

The word **mannerism** refers to specific, habitual actions that often characterize people. Such actions as rubbing the elbows, tugging at an earlobe, and licking the lips are examples. These kinds of actions can do a great deal to make your characters seem realistic. Of course, such mannerisms can be overdone; but selectively used, they can do much to help you create distinctive, realistic human beings. Some interpreters like to use a specific mannerism to distinguish each character. This specific action is called that character's **master gesture.** When the audience sees that mannerism, they know immediately which character is speaking. A master gesture can play an important part in character distinction. As a matter of fact, you can create a catalogue of such mannerisms by observing people in public places, such as shopping malls. If you keep a written record of what you observe, you will have a storehouse of possible mannerisms that you can use, as appropriate, for future characterizations. The master gesture, though, should never become a mere pose. Don't fall into the trap of playing an attitude rather than becoming a full character.

Pantomime is the use of physical actions to imitate business carried out in real life. For example, if you were to go through all the motions of washing your face without using soap, a washcloth, or water, you would be using pantomime. This kind of action is sometimes necessary and useful in interpretation. For instance, if you were to interpret a scene from the play *The Dresser* by Ronald Harwood, it would be important for the audience to understand that the character Sir, an aging actor, is putting on stage makeup while he speaks his lines. Yet the lines alone do not make it clear what Sir is doing moment by moment. In this instance pantomime is appropriate, perhaps even essential.

Any pantomimed actions should be clear, accurately and economically carried out, and used only where necessary. Interpretation is not an exhibition of pantomime skills, but the performer with such skills can use them to advantage when they are necessary. Usually you are better off suggesting actions rather than enacting them in such detail that they call attention to themselves. For example, if two characters shake hands, you need not go through the exact motions by putting out your hand, clasping the air, and shaking it. Rather you can suggest the action by extending the hand. Only when a suggestion of the action would not be clear to the audience should you resort to detailed pantomime.

It has been said that the essence of art is contrast. This is an important principle to remember as you develop your physical characterizations. An audience at a play has no difficulty telling the characters apart because they are played by different actors. In interpretation, however, the same performer plays all the roles. As the performer, you can use a number of contrasting qualities to keep your characters from seeming too similar. Through a number of bodily adjustments, you can make them have distinctive physical appearances. Posture is one possibility: one character might have erect posture while another slouches. You can also show contrast through general body tensions: one character might be loose and relaxed while the other is uptight and tense. In addition, eye focus can create a sense of different heights. If one character looks up slightly while speaking and the other character looks down slightly, the audience will perceive that a tall and a short character are speaking together.

Earlier you saw how distinctive mannerisms may also help to distinguish characters. Contrasting facial expressions can help as well. Often it's helpful to spend some time in front of a mirror while experimenting with contrasting body movements and facial expressions. Doing so can enable you to find diverse physical appearances for your characters.

You can get strong contrasts through vocal adjustments. You can contrast **rate,** or the speed of speaking; **volume,** the loudness or softness of the speech; **pitch,** the highness or lowness of sound on a musical scale; **timbre,** the richness of the sound; and **quality,** that distinctive aspect of a voice that makes it different from all others. In addition, some characters have sharp articulation while others do not; some speak with dialects; some have distinctive traits such as speech defects or particular mannerisms of speech; some pause frequently; some have vocal patterns. So many possibilities for contrasting character voices exist that you should always be able to create very distinctive voices. Just be certain the voice you create fits the character. Use a tape recorder and play with the variations you can create. There is no limit to the range of possibilities.

Activity 1   Creating Character Shifts

1. From the list of suggested characters, select two and prepare to deliver the short dialogue that follows. Either character may be A; the other will be B. Or if you prefer you can write your own thirty-second dialogue and deliver it. Work to create different gestures, mannerisms, and vocal qualities for the characters so that the contrast between them is clear. Then present the dialogue from memory to demonstrate your ability to characterize effectively.

a Southern lady/gentleman	a society lady/gentleman
a streetwise teenager	a country yokel
a foreigner who just arrived in the U.S.	a person with a cold
an elderly person	an elf
a nervous person	a shy person
a person from New York City	a gypsy
a T.V. game-show host	a character you create

A: Excuse me, but I think I'm lost. Can you help me?

B: Do I look like a cop or something? I'm a stranger here myself.

A: I'm sorry. I thought that maybe you lived in this area.

B: No. I live across town. I'm on my way to Nelson's Coffee Shop on the corner of Tenth and Sycamore. If you'd like, you can come along and maybe someone there can help you.

A: That's a good idea. Thank you for suggesting it. Which way?

B: That way. Just follow me. And don't be too slow.

2. As a class or in groups, discuss the performances. Point out those qualities that made the characters distinct and individual. If some of the characters didn't seem believable or interesting, suggest what could be done to make them more effective. Take turns experimenting with characterization as you work. ■

Dealing with Details

According to the great Russian acting teacher Konstantin Stanislavski, "*in general* is the enemy of art." He urged actors to use specific details in preparing their characterizations. His advice applies as well to oral interpreters. Attention to detail is the mark of a good interpreter, and that attention is important during both preparation and performance. Sometimes paying attention to detail involves research, perhaps a trip to the library reference department.

Paying attention to detail is imperative in rehearsal to find the right way to pantomime an action or time a line for maximum effect. This aspect is particularly important in the interpretation of humorous drama, where timing is essential for pointing up humor. You might say a line numerous ways until you find the one that works best; you might try a number of ways of using a gesture or a look to punctuate a line until you find the most effective manner.

Attending to detail is also important in performance because an otherwise good presentation may be ruined by a careless moment. An audience can sense almost immediately whether the performer is truly involved in her or his scene or is merely running through the performance in a mechanical way that some call being "on automatic pilot." To avoid such a trap, you must take a few minutes before every performance to prepare for the event. Begin by taking some deep breaths to relax your body, closing your eyes and imagining the environment you want to create, and summoning up the energy needed to make a dynamic presentation. This preliminary ritual is important if you want consistently to present your best possible performance.

Once into a performance, you need to play the scene moment-by-moment without allowing any detail of intention, characterization, or technical skill to be slighted. Every audience deserves your best efforts, and no performer can give her or his best without attending to each detail as the performance unfolds. It's easy after you have rehearsed a scene and performed it numerous times to let your mind wander to later parts of the selection, what's happening out in the hallway, or even things you have to do after the performance. Such lapses in concentration are dangerous. The only way to avoid them and maintain spontaneity is to keep your mind on what's happening at each moment.

Finding the Focus

Chapter 4 mentioned the use of **focal points,** those spots where the speaking characters visualize the listening characters. These are the points to which the speaker directs energy just as if conversing with a real person at each spot. As you shift to another character, you should also shift to another focal point. Otherwise the audience may have trouble distinguishing your characters. The diagrams that follow may help you understand this concept.

Dual Character Focal Points

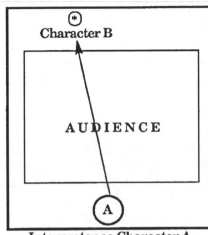

Interpreter as Character A
Speaking to Character B

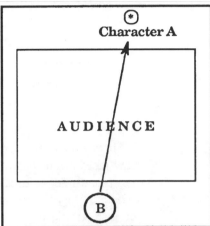

Interpreter as Character B
Speaking to Character A

Select your focal points carefully as their placement will affect your performance. The points should be placed just enough above the heads of the audience that the speaking character does not make direct eye contact with an audience member. The spot needs to be located just beyond the back of the audience so that even those in the last row can feel they are seated in the midst of the scene. Also, you may want to adjust the angle of focus just a bit, depending on the relative heights of the characters: a short character or one supposedly seated, as Kistunov is at some points in "A Defenseless Creature," would look up slightly to meet the eyes of a taller person just as the taller person would look down slightly to meet the eyes of the shorter or seated character. Be careful not to exaggerate these angles. You don't want to give the impression that your scene involves pygmies talking to giants!

Likewise, don't let the focal points be too far apart. Too much distance between them can slow down the scene when you shift characters, or it can make a performer interpreting short, quick exchanges look like a sports fan at a fast-paced tennis match. The exact angle used will depend on the number of characters and the size of your audience. If one character speaks to several listening characters, you must place each one at a slightly different point and make a slight eye and/or head adjustment to suggest that you've shifted your attention to another person. The following diagram may help you understand this concept.

Multiple Character Focal Points

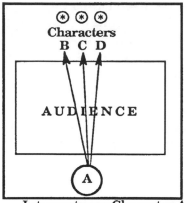

Interpreter as Character A
Speaking to Characters B, C, D

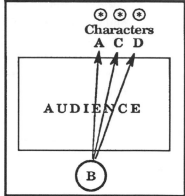

Interpreter as Character B
Speaking to Characters A, C, D

It is important to make certain you are talking to a person, not just a piece of spot. Draw faces or cut out magazine pictures representing the characters in your selection and then tape these pictures on the back wall at the appropriate focal points. Seeing a face may be helpful to you, but remember that a real person looking at you would be responding, not just staring in frozen silence. In the end, the only way you can suggest real human interaction is to be able to imagine a living, reacting face at each focal point, with or without a picture there.

Activity 2   Using Focal Points

1. Improvise a scene with three contrasting characters. Pretend you are Character A. You are speaking to Character B and Character C. Character B is slightly taller than you are. Character C is seated. Think of something brief you want to say to Character B and then something to say to Character C. Pick out focal points and practice speaking what you have to say until you feel comfortable working with focal points.

2. Now take the role of Character B and speak to Character A and Character C. Again, work with focal points until you are comfortable and can handle the shifts effectively. ■

Establishing the Environment

That "you can't act in a vacuum" is as true an adage for the interpreter as it is for the actor. Every event happens in some location, and that location or environment affects the action. For example, studies by both law officials and psychologists show that violence and crime increase as the temperature rises and as areas become more crowded. You've probably noticed that the weather affects your moods and that you feel and behave differently depending on whether you're in an enclosed space or a wide-open field.

Even though our surroundings greatly affect our actions and moods, playwrights usually do not provide detailed word pictures of the scene; they rarely provide the elaborate descriptions created by many writers of prose fiction. Playwrights prefer to give brief hints and allow the scenic designers to enrich their concepts through detailed settings, such as those you have seen on stages, on television, and in movies. As the interpreter, you are also the set designer; and you must envision and build the environment in the imaginations of yourself and your audiences. How do you accomplish such a task? The first step is to make the scene real for yourself.

Begin with what the playwright gives you and let your imagination go from there. If the author tells you only that the scene is a park on a summer night, you must supply the details. Does moonlight filter through the trees, or is the night very dark? Is it quiet, or is the air filled with the sounds of night birds, crickets, and locusts? Is the air cool, or is it hot and humid? Do the trees seem peaceful and protective, or are they looming and ominous? Once you have thought out a detailed setting—including the sounds and smells of the place—you are ready to move on.

The second step is relatively easy. Imagine yourself—as the characters, of course—in that environment. Can you see, hear, smell, taste, and feel it? Can you create it in your mind repeatedly as you rehearse the scene? Only if it is absolutely real to you can you hope to make it real for your audience.

Finally, decide on actions you can do to suggest the environment to your audience. For example, if the weather is hot and humid, observe people's reactions to such conditions and use them in your performance. Might you at some time wipe perspiration from your face, fan yourself, or slow down your movements? If you need to convey a smell, perhaps you could sniff and then show by your reaction whether the odor is the fresh fragrance of jasmine or the pungent perfume of skunk. The importance of a sound can sometimes be conveyed by turning your head slightly and listening intently. You can often suggest the size and mood of a space by the character's eye focus. Simply the way a character looks at something can tell a great deal about what she or he is seeing—the type and size of the object, its particular placement or location, its distance from the character. For example, if you are portraying a character entering a room he or she has never seen before, your eyes need to see each piece of furniture, the wallpaper, the pictures—everything. In this way the audience will see the surroundings through you.

Of course these matters must not be overdone; but through a vivid imagination, strong concentration, and appropriate physical reactions, you can convey to your audience the environment in which a scene is played.

Activity 3   Creating an Environment

1. Choose a sport, event, or activity that you can observe and that is characterized by specific actions and sounds, something such as a tennis match, a rock concert, or a dance. Standing before a group or the entire class, watch that sport, event, or activity as though it were taking place just beyond the back of your audience. Don't jump up and down or rely on pantomimed actions. Just watch and listen. See specific actions as they unfold before you and hear specific sounds. Don't say anything; just let your reactions develop naturally. After one minute, see if your audience can tell what you were watching.

2. After a number of individuals have done the watching and listening exercise, point out specific actions that made clear what they were seeing and/or hearing. What made the actions of some clearer than those of others? What additional responses might have communicated these environments more effectively about their environment? ■

Plotting the Progression

In order to hold an audience's attention, a scene and its characters need to develop. When a scene has a sense of forward movement and when characters change moment by moment as they respond to each other, the audience knows the performance is alive and that anything may happen. You can achieve this sense of spontaneity in a number of ways.

First, keep your attention on the characters' conflicting intentions. Line by line a character must listen to and adjust to others just as a good athlete constantly watches and reacts to an opponent's every move. Two opposing characters really committed to achieving their intentions and concentrating on their efforts create a tension that grips audiences. Such characters are **dynamic,** not **static;** they develop and grow rather than just exist.

Second, pick up your cues; that is, shift from character to character quickly enough that there is no lag time—not even a second—when you let down the tension. Because such quick shifts are crucial, some interpreters have referred to them as **pops** from one character to another. Indeed, you must let every aspect of your physical characterization—body tension, focal point, facial expression, and gesture—snap from one characterization to the other. Such an instruction does not mean that you should avoid pauses; rather it means you should not pause when you are changing characters. When you pause, do so while in character, keeping all physical aspects of the characterization.

You can pick up your cues with either a look or a word. The important point is that you commit yourself totally to the shift. Doing it halfway will not suffice. Almost always the facial and bodily reactions come slightly *before* the words when you make character shifts. That way your audience sees the new character hearing and reacting to what has just been said *before* the character utters a word in response.

Third, move each episode to a climax. As characters oppose each other, each tries to dominate or top the other. The result is a gradual increase in the volume and speed of their interaction. Finally one of them wins a point and the tension eases slightly as the two get ready to begin another round. For example, notice this little episode in the conflict between Kistunov and the woman:

Woman:	Are you saying you won't believe my husband is sick? Here! Here is a doctor's certificate. There's the proof. Do you still doubt that my husband is suffering from a nervous disorder?
Kistunov:	Not only do I not doubt it, I would *swear* to it.
Woman:	*Look at it! You didn't look at it!*
Kistunov:	It's really not necessary. I know *full well* how your husband must be suffering.
Woman:	*What's the point in a doctor's certificate if you don't look at it?!* LOOK AT IT!

Each character builds the argument to a climax by nearly cutting off the other's speeches and trying to top the other speaker's volume and energy. Notice that the woman wins this short battle, for Kistunov finally looks at the paper as she has demanded. Next they begin to build another little unit of conflict to another climax. Gradually these minor climaxes build to the moment Kistunov screams, "STOP!" and agrees to give the woman everything she wants.

Finally, aid a scene's progression by your reactions. Dramatic events happen *now,* not in the past tense. Each moment seems fresh, and each action seems to some degree unexpected. Thus the characters are a little surprised by the unfolding of each moment. Show with your facial expression each character's spontaneous reaction to the unfolding situation.

Especially let a character show that he or she has made a *discovery*. If your reactions are clear and sharp, you will keep a scene fresh no matter how many times you have rehearsed or performed it.

Activity 4   Building a Climax

1. Using "A Defenseless Creature," one of the selections at the end of this chapter, or a play of your own choosing, find a one-minute sequence between two characters that builds to a climax. Working from a script, read the sequence to show these characters attempting to top each other. Pick up cues and gradually increase the volume. After you have rehearsed the scene, read it to a partner, a group, or the entire class.

2. Discuss the performances you observe, giving feedback to help each performer know how distinct the characters seemed, how sharply cues were picked up, and how effectively the scene built toward its moment of climax. ■

Cutting, Dialect, and the Sound of Silence

As you prepare a drama scene for performance, you will have to make choices about a number of matters external to the scene itself. One decision is whether or not to memorize the scene. Of course, you must do what your teacher assigns or follow the rules of the particular contest in which you are competing. If the choice is entirely yours, what should your decision be? Because the interpretation of drama often involves more physical actions than the interpretation of prose fiction or poetry, you may wish to free your hands from the script. But even if you choose to use a manuscript—as you generally must in duo interpretations of drama, you must have the script nearly memorized. If you don't, you cannot make quick character pops. Although you may not weaken the performance if your eyes drop to the script from time to time *during* speeches, you must not glance down *between* speeches. Even a quick glance at that crucial time will slow the cues and cause the tension of the scene to lag. For this reason many interpreters feel drama scenes should be performed from memory.

A second decision you must make is whether or not to cut a selection for performance. As mentioned in Chapter 4, it is usually better to present a complete excerpt than a scene with a significant amount of internal cutting. Good playwrights develop their scenes and speeches with such precise progressions that any cutting can destroy their subtle builds or eliminate key elements of motivation. Once lines are cut, characters' intentions can become unclear or change completely from what they originally were. Whether you choose an excerpt or a scene condensed through cutting, be sure it has a clear progression with conflicts rising to a climax.

Another decision you must often make is whether or not to use a dialect, or accent, for one of the characters. If a script indicates that a character has a dialect, it is probably best to use one. In the absence of any special indication, you will need to use your own discretion. You should not use a dialect just for the sake of the dialect itself. Even if a play is set in France, for instance, you would not be required to use a French dialect. If all characters come from the same area, the dialect may be unnecessary, perhaps even confusing.

Sometimes, however, using a dialect may add an effective element. If you are skilled at using dialects, you might consider using them to perform "A Defenseless Creature." Kistunov's name suggests he may be effective with a Russian dialect, and the woman's lines have the lilt of a Yiddish dialect. The contrast of the dialects could emphasize the great contrasts between the two characters. On the other hand, using two dialects in the same selection is very difficult. If you can't do a dialect consistently and accurately, or if the dialect interferes with the audiences's understanding of the words, it's better not to use it at all. If you cannot master a dialect required for a character, such as the Cockney Eliza Doolittle in Bernard Shaw's *Pygmalion,* then select another piece of literature.

Those interested in using dialects should check with a teacher or a library to see if dialect tapes are available.

A final consideration is how often to use pauses or silences in your performance. Beginning interpreters tend to undervalue pauses, almost as if they are afraid of the silence. Actually, silence used effectively can be an interpreter's best friend. In real life at moments of powerful emotional intensity, people often can't find the words to express their feelings: They are speechless. At the opposite extreme, sometimes our silent reactions are so strong that we just freeze. Such moments are often very funny. Think about times you've seen a television comic just hold a look—sometimes called a **take**—for a long moment while the audience howls with laughter. During the silences in an interpretive performance, the audience has the time to be stunned by an emotional situation and respond to it, or to catch a joke and laugh at it.

The interpreter who can use pauses effectively—but not excessively—can make a very strong impact on his or her audience. However, be careful to avoid some potential pitfalls. First, be certain pauses come in the right places. A pause *before* a word creates suspense, as in, "And the murderer is . . . the butler." A pause *after* a word creates emphasis. An inappropriate pause in the middle of a phrase, however, merely interrupts the idea and the flow of the scene.

Second, be sure pauses are *filled* with something—usually suspense, uncertainty, or reflection. For example, if one person hits another, there is a moment of uncertainty when neither the audience nor the character who was hit knows if he or she will hit back or run away. The audience holds its breath in anticipation. Interestingly, if the interpreter also holds a quick breath at that time, the silence will seem that much more compelling; a silence held on exhalation seems dead and dull.

Concentrating on Commitment

Commitment to your scene and characters is very important if you want to create a memorable performance. Many interpreters present lukewarm scenes even though they do all the steps of preparation well and rehearse properly. The reason: they do not carry commitment into the performance. **Commitment** means involving yourself totally and energetically in your actions. The characters in the scene you perform must be committed to achieving their intentions, to winning the encounters with their opponents; and you must be committed to conveying all mental, emotional, and physical aspects of the scene to your audience.

To achieve commitment you need to master three things. First, you must know the scene and the characters so well that you can perform with confidence. You can't communicate what you don't know. Without something to share with an audience, you have nothing to be committed to. Second, you must focus your energy and actions so that your performance is direct and sharp with no unnecessary actions or weaknesses in delivery to distract the audience. Third, you need performance energy to project the words and emotions to the entire audience. If you are determined to make a strong commitment of mind, body, and energy, you can have a tremendous impact on an audience as you create a scene and share with them a moving human experience.

Activity 5   Putting It All Together

1. Several drama selections follow. Study at least three to gain experience using the techniques discussed in Chapters 7 and 8.

FROM ROMEO AND JULIET

by William Shakespeare

This story of star-crossed lovers traces the struggle of Romeo and Juliet to escape a bitter quarrel between their two families in order to find happiness together. After having met and fallen in love with her young lover on the evening of a dance, Juliet impatiently waits in Act II, Scene V, for her nurse to bring word from Romeo about plans for their secret marriage. The nurse, however, delights in delaying the news.

Juliet: The clock struck nine when I did send the nurse;
In half an hour she promised to return.
Perchance she cannot meet him. That's not so.
O, she is lame! Love's heralds should be thoughts,
Which ten times faster glide than the sun's beams
Driving back shadows over low'ring hills.
Therefore do nimble-pinioned doves draw Love,
And therefore hath the wind-swift Cupid wings.
Now is the sun upon the highmost hill
Of this day's journey, and from nine till twelve
Is three long hours; yet she is not come.
Had she affections and warm youthful blood,
She would be as swift in motion as a ball;
My words would bandy her to my sweet love,
And his to me.
But old folks, many feign as they were dead—
Unwieldy, slow, heavy and pale as lead.

Enter Nurse.

O God, she comes! O honey nurse, what news?
Has thou met with him?—O Lord, why lookest thou sad?
Though news be sad, yet tell them merrily;
If good, thou shamest the music of sweet news
By playing it to me with so sour a face.

Nurse: I am aweary, give me leave awhile.
Fie, how my bones ache! What a jaunce have I had!

Juliet: I would thou hadst my bones, and I thy news.
Nay, come, I pray thee speak. Good, good nurse, speak.

Nurse: Jesu, what haste! Can you not stay awhile?
Do you not see that I am out of breath?

Juliet: How art thou out of breath when thou hast breath
To say to me that thou art out of breath?
The excuse that thou dost make in this delay
Is longer than the tale thou dost excuse.
Is thy news good or bad? Answer to that.
Say either, and I'll stay the circumstance.
Let me be satisfied, is't good or bad?

Nurse: Well, you have made a simple choice; you know not how to choose a man. Romeo? No, not he. Though his face be better than any man's, yet his leg excels all men's; and for a hand and a foot, and a body, though they be not to be talked on, yet they are past compare. He is not the flower of courtesy, but, I'll warrant him, as gentle as a lamb. Go they ways, wench; serve God. What, have you dined at home?

Juliet: No, no. But all this did I know before.
What says he of our marriage? What of that?

Nurse: Lord, how my head aches! What a head have I!
It beats as it would fall in twenty pieces.
My back a t'other side—ah, my back, my back!*
Beshrew your heart for sending me about
To catch my death with jauncing up and down!

Juliet: I'faith, I am sorry that thou art not well.
Sweet, sweet, sweet nurse, tell me, what says my love?

Nurse: Your love says, like an honest gentleman, and a courteous, and a kind, and a handsome, and I warrant, a virtuous—Where is your mother?

Juliet: Where is my mother? Why, she is within.
Where should she be? How oddly thou repliest!
"Your love says, like an honest gentleman,
'Where is your mother?' "

Nurse: O God's Lady dear!
Are you so hot? Marry come up, I trow.
Is this the poultice for my aching bones?
Henceforward do your messages yourself.

Juliet: Here's such a coil! Come, what says Romeo?

Nurse: Have you got leave to go to shrift to-day?

Juliet: I have.

Nurse: Then hie you hence to Friar Laurence' cell;
There stays a husband to make you a wife.
Now comes the wanton blood up in your cheeks;
They'll be in scarlet straight at any news.
Hie you to church; I must another way,
To fetch a ladder, by the which your love
Must climb a bird's nest soon when it is dark.
I am the drudge, and toil in your delight;
But you shall bear the burden soon at night.
Go; I'll to dinner; hie you to the cell.

Juliet: Hie to high fortune! Honest nurse, farewell.

---

* To encourage her nurse to tell her what she wants to know, Juliet is rubbing the woman's back.

Getting Started in Oral Interpretation

Dino

by Reginald Rose

Rose's play, *Dino,* set in the mid 1950s, is the study of a troubled family and the effect the loss of family has on seventeen-year-old Dino Falcaro, a young man trapped in anger and loneliness. Mr. Sheridan is the dedicated, overburdened caseworker who want to get Dino to open up and trust him. Dino is determined to hide his experiences and feelings from Sheridan.

Sheridan: Hello, Dino.

(Dino stands at the door, hands in his jacket pockets.)

Dino: I'm not comin' back here no more. (Mr. Sheridan *shows no surprise, but sits and waits.* Dino *is angry.)* So why don't you say somethin' when I say somethin'? I said I'm not comin' back here no more. So what about it?

Sheridan: I think you need to come here, Dino.

Dino: I need nothin'.

(He paces to the window. The blinds are lowered.)

Sheridan: *(Carefully.)* Did something happen last night, Dino?

Dino: *(Fast.)* No!

Sheridan: Well, what are you so angry about? Nothin's happened in here yet. You haven't even taken off your jacket. *(There is a pause.* Dino *turns away from* Mr. Sheridan, *who speaks quietly.)* How's your brother?

Dino: *(Still angry.)* What do you care?

Sheridan: I thought maybe you were angry at *him.*

Dino: *(Loud.)* No, I'm not, genius! *(There is a pause.* Mr. Sheridan *waits. Finally* Dino *turns to* Mr. Sheridan.) I'm angry at you!

Sheridan: Why?

Dino: *(Loud.)* Because you're sittin' there with your face hangin' out, waitin' for me to say stuff I don't wanna say.

Sheridan: Why don't you want to say it?

Dino: *(Shouting.)* Because! *(There is a pause.)* I don't know. *(Mr. Sheridan* waits. *Slowly* Dino *walks over to the desk and sits down. He picks up the paper weight and toys with it. When he finally speaks his voice is strained, low, tormented. This is sheer torture for him. He begins to squirm in the chair halfway through the lines, becoming more and more anxious as he speaks. He faces the floor most of the time.)* Like it's everybody's business. Why don't you mind *your* business? Makin' me come in here. What do you want to know so much for? *(He looks at* Mr. Sheridan.) It's too hot in here. *(He looks down at the floor getting no response.)* Stinkin' little room. Like sittin' in jail! I wasn't gonna come here at all. I just came to tell you that, and that's all you're gettin' outa me. *(He looks up at* Mr. Sheridan.) What're ya lookin' at? Stop fatherin' me! *(Then he realizes his slip.)* Stop botherin' me! *(Mr. Sheridan* doesn't respond. Dino *looks down at the floor.)* I made him smack me last night. So what! That's all he wants, anyway. He can't hurt me; he could never hurt me in my whole life.

Sheridan: *(Softly.)* Who?

Dino: *(Low.)* You know who. My old man.

Sheridan: *(Softly.)* He never hurt you?

Dino: *(Speaking to himself.)* Never! Because I'm tough. He can smack me forever. I'm too tough. *(There is a pause.)* Even when I was little—I never cried. I'm tellin' ya. He could knock out my teeth. Anything!—I wouldn't cry. *(Another pause.)* What'd he want to hit me all the time for?—The dirty bum! On my birthday once. The dirty, lousy bum. I yelled at him because he forgot to give me a present. A million other times. When I was little— wow, I was scared! Like there was nothin' in the world but him, like a giant. He never did nothin' for me. So I never cried for him. And I never will. *(His voice goes lower and lower, and he turns and twists, staring at the floor. It is as though* Mr. Sheridan *is no longer there.)* I don't remember anyone kissed me, ever. So what? All they wanted was me outa there. Him and my mother. So I got outa there. Boy, that's what they wanted! So I got into reform school. How come nobody ever kissed me? They wanted me outa there. *(His voice begins to break.)* That dirty, rotten bum! He never took me anywhere. He never fooled around with me, or gave me bear hugs. Nothin'. He didn't want me. He didn't want to see me. Just to hit. But I never cried! I never cried! I never cried! *(And suddenly he is in tears, sobbing violently, head down on the desk, close to hysteria, crying out the pain as if he will never stop.* Mr. Sheridan *watches him quietly. Slowly his sobbing begins to stop. Finally, after a long while, he raises his head. He is much too ashamed to look at* Mr. Sheridan. Mr. Sheridan *hands him a kleenex. He brushes it away.)*

Sheridan: *(Gently.)* Most people cry in here. It's a very normal, natural thing to do, Dino. *(Dino turns away in shame.)* I think you were crying for all the times you wanted to cry when you were small. Tears make people feel better sometimes; they're nothing to be ashamed of.

(Dino finally manages to look at Mr. Sheridan.*)*

Dino: *(Angry.)* You made me . . .

Sheridan: No one made you, Dino; you just couldn't help it. Like maybe your father just can't help being the way he is, or your mother. Because just the way their emotional problems helped make you what you are, so did their parents' problems affect them, and theirs them. This is the way it is, Dino. No one's really to blame. So many people just aren't equipped to be people. Just, no matter how sad and unfair it seems, don't blame your mother and father too much. They have a very hard time, just trying to stay alive and well and reasonably unafraid. Don't expect too much from them. They just haven't got it to give. Maybe after a while you'll understand that, and adjust to it. I hope so, Dino.

(During these lines Dino *has been staring at the wall, but he's listened. Now he stands up and walks to the window.)*

Dino: *(Still shaken.)* I want to go now.

Sheridan: Whenever you like.

Dino: And I'm not comin' back. I'm not goin' through that again.

Sheridan: *(Gently.)* It's hard. Getting face to face with yourself is one of the toughest things you'll ever do, Dino. But it's worth it.

Dino: I don't want to listen to you. I'm gettin' out of here! *(He strides to the door and opens it.)*

Sheridan: Same time tomorrow, Dino.

Dino: *(Angry.)* I said I'm not comin' back! Are you deaf or somethin'?

from Joe Turner's Come and Gone
by August Wilson

Zonia is the eleven-year-old daughter of Harold Loomis, a man who has just served seven years' hard labor on Joe Turner's chain gang. Now he and his daughter are in Pittsburgh at a boardinghouse. Loomis wants to find his wife, hoping she can help him reclaim his life. Zonia is searching for life, too, and she meets and becomes friends with Reuben, a boy who lives in the neighborhood and looks after the pigeons that once belonged to his friend Eugene.

The lights come up on Zonia *and* Reuben *in the yard.*

Reuben: Something spookly going on around here. Last night Mr. Bynum was out in the yard singing and talking to the wind . . . and the wind it just be talking back to him. Did you hear it?

Zonia: I heard it. I was scared to get up and look. I thought it was a storm.

Reuben: That wasn't no storm. That was Mr. Bynum. First he say something . . . and the wind it say back to him.

Zonia: I heard it. Was you scared? I was scared.

Reuben: And then this morning . . . I seen Miss Mabel!

Zonia: Who Miss Mabel?

Reuben: Mr. Seth's mother. He got her picture hanging up in the house. She been dead.

Zonia: How you seen her if she been dead?

Reuben: Zonia . . . if I tell you something you promise you won't tell anybody?

Zonia: I promise.

Reuben: It was early this morning . . . I went out to the coop to feed the pigeons. I was down on the ground like this to open up the door to the coop . . . when all of a sudden I seen some feets in front of me. I looked up . . . and there was Miss Mabel standing there.

Zonia: Reuben, you better stop telling that! You ain't seen nobody!

Reuben: Naw, it's the truth. I swear! I seen her just like I see you. Look . . . you can see where she hit me with her cane.

Zonia: Hit you? What she hit you for?

Reuben: She says, "Didn't you promise Eugene something?" Then she hit me with her cane. She say, "Let them pigeons go." Then she hit me again. That's what made them marks.

Zonia: Jeez man . . . get away from me. You done see a haunt!

Reuben: Shhhh. You promised, Zonia!

Zonia: You sure it wasn't Miss Bertha come over there and hit you with her hoe?

Reuben: It wasn't no Miss Bertha. I told you it was Miss Mabel. She was standing right here by the coop. She had this light coming out of her and then she just melted away.

Zonia: What she had on?

Reuben: A white dress. Ain't even had no shoes or nothing. Just had on that white dress and them big hands . . . and that cane she hit me with.

Zonia: How you reckon she knew about the pigeons? You reckon Eugene told her?

Reuben: I don't know. I sure ain't asked her none. She say Eugene was waiting on them pigeons. Say he couldn't go back home till I let them go. I couldn't get the door to the coop open fast enough.

Zonia:	Maybe she an angel? From the way you say she look with that white dress. Maybe she an angel.
Reuben:	Mean as she was . . . how she gonna be an angel? She used to chase us out her yard and frown up and look evil all the time.
Zonia:	That don't mean she can't be no angel 'cause of how she looked and 'cause she wouldn't let no kids play in her yard. It go by if you got any spots on your heart and if you pray and go to church.
Reuben:	What about she hit me with her cane? An angel wouldn't hit me with her cane.
Zonia:	I don't know. She might. I still say she was an angel.
Reuben:	You reckon Eugene the one who sent old Miss Mabel?
Zonia:	Why he send her? Why he don't come himself?
Reuben:	Figured if he send her maybe that'll make me listen. 'Cause she old.
Zonia:	What you think it feel like?
Reuben:	What?
Zonia:	Being dead.
Reuben:	Like being sleep only you don't know nothing and can't move no more.
Zonia:	If Miss Mabel can come back . . . then maybe Eugene can come back too.
Reuben:	We can go down to the hideout like we used to! He could come back everyday! It be just like he ain't dead.
Zonia:	Maybe that ain't right for him to come back. Feel kinda funny to be playing games with a haunt.
Reuben:	Yeah . . . what if everybody came back? What if Miss Mabel came back just like she ain't dead? Where you and your daddy gonna sleep then?
Zonia:	Maybe they go back at night and don't need no place to sleep.
Reuben:	It still don't seem right. I'm sure gonna miss Eugene. He's the bestest friend anybody ever had.
Zonia:	My daddy say if you miss somebody too much it can kill you. Say he missed me till it liked to killed him.
Reuben:	What if your mama's already dead and all the time you looking for her?
Zonia:	Naw, she ain't dead. My daddy say he can smell her.
Reuben:	You can't smell nobody that ain't here. Maybe he smelling old Miss Bertha. Maybe Miss Bertha be your mama?
Zonia:	Naw, she ain't. My mama got long pretty hair and she five feet from the ground.
Reuben:	Your daddy say when you leaving? *(Zonia doesn't respond.)* Maybe you gonna stay in Mr. Seth's house and don't go looking for your mama no more.
Zonia:	He say we got to leave on Saturday.
Reuben:	Dag! You just only been here for a little while. Don't seem like nothing ever stay the same.

FROM ANDROCLES AND THE LION

by Bernard Shaw

The Prologue of Shaw's fable-play introduces Androcles, his overbearing wife Megaera, and an almost "human" lion with a thorn in his paw. Androcles has an opportunity to rescue the lion from his pain; later, the lion will rescue Androcles when he's sent to die in the Roman Arena. But no one, it seems, can rescue Megaera from the frustration of life with her husband.

Megaera: *(suddenly throwing down her stick)* I won't go another step.

Androcles: *(pleading wearily)* Oh, not again, dear. What's the good of stopping every two miles and saying you won't go another step? We must get on to the next village before night. There are wild beasts in this wood: lions, they say.

Megaera: I don't believe a word of it. You are always threatening me with wild beasts to make me walk the very soul out of my body when I can hardly drag one foot before another. We haven't seen a single lion yet.

Androcles: Well, dear, do you want to see one?

Megaera: *(tearing the bundle from his back)* You cruel brute, you don't care how tired I am, or what becomes of me *(she throws the bundle on the ground)* always thinking of yourself. Self! self! self! always yourself! *(She sits down on the bundle.)*

Androcles: *(sitting down sadly on the ground with his elbows on his knees and his head in his hands)* We all have to think of ourselves occasionally, dear.

Megaera: A man ought to think of his wife sometimes.

Androcles: He can't always help it, dear. You make me think of you a good deal. Not that I blame you.

Megaera: Blame me! I should think not indeed. Is it my fault that I'm married to you?

Androcles: No, dear: that is my fault.

Megaera: That's a nice thing to say to me. Aren't you happy with me?

Androcles: I don't complain, my love.

Megaera: You ought to be ashamed of yourself.

Androcles: I am, my dear.

Megaera: You're not: you glory in it.

Androcles: In what, darling?

Megaera: In everything. In making me a slave, and making yourself a laughingstock. It's not fair. You get me the name of being a shrew with your meek ways, always talking as if butter wouldn't melt in your mouth. And just because I look a big strong woman, and because I'm good-hearted and a bit hasty, and because you're always driving me to do things I'm sorry for afterwards, people say "Poor man: what a life his wife leads him!" Oh, if they only knew! And you think I don't know. But I do, I do, *(screaming)* I do.

Androcles: Yes, my dear: I know you do.

Megaera: Then why don't you treat me properly and be a good husband to me?

Androcles: What can I do, my dear?

Megaera: What can you do! You can return to your duty, and come back to your home and your friends, and sacrifice to the gods as all respectable people do, instead of having us hunted out of house and home for being dirty disreputable blaspheming atheists.

Androcles:	I'm not an atheist, dear: I am a Christian.
Megaera:	Well, isn't that the same thing, only ten times worse? Everybody knows that the Christians are the lowest of the low.
Androcles:	Just like us, dear.
Megaera:	Speak for yourself. Don't you dare to compare me to common people. My father owned his own public-house; and sorrowful was the day for me when you first came drinking in our bar.
Androcles:	I confess I was addicted to it, dear. But I gave it up when I became a Christian.
Megaera:	You'd much better have remained a drunkard. I can forgive a man being addicted to drink: it's only natural; and I don't deny I like a drop myself sometimes. What I can't stand is your being addicted to Christianity. And what's worse again, your being addicted to animals. How is any woman to keep her house clean when you bring in every stray cat and lost cur and lame duck in the whole countryside? You took the bread out of my mouth to feed them: you know you did: don't attempt to deny it.
Androcles:	Only when they were hungry and you were getting too stout, dearie.
Megaera:	Yes: insult me, do. *(Rising)* Oh! I won't bear it another moment. You used to sit and talk to those dumb brute beasts for hours, when you hadn't a word for me.
Androcles:	They never answered back, darling. *(He rises and again shoulders the bundle.)*
Megaera:	Well, if you're fonder of animals than of your own wife, you can live with them here in the jungle. I've had enough of them and of you. I'm going back. I'm going home.
Androcles:	*(barring the way back)* No, dearie: don't take on like that. We can't go back. We've sold everything: we should starve; and I should be sent to Rome and thrown to the lions—
Megaera:	Serve you right! I wish the lions joy of you. *(Screaming)* Are you going to get out of my way and let me go home?
Androcles:	No, dear—
Megaera:	Then I'll make my way through the forest; and when I'm eaten by the wild beasts you'll know what a wife you've lost. *(She dashes into the jungle and nearly falls over the sleeping lion.)* Oh! Oh! Andy! Andy! *(She totters back and collapses into the arms of Androcles, who, crushed by her weight, falls on his bundle.)*
Androcles:	*(extracting himself from beneath her and slapping her hands in great anxiety)* What is it, my precious, my pet? What's the matter? *(He raises her head. Speechless with terror, she points in the direction of the sleeping lion. He steals cautiously towards the spot indicated by Megaera. She rises with an effort and totters after him.)*
Megaera:	Now, Andy: you'll be killed. Come back.
	(The lion utters a long snoring sigh. Androcles sees the lion, and recoils fainting into the arms of Megaera, who falls back on the bundle. They roll apart and lie staring in terror at one another. The lion is heard groaning heavily in the jungle.)
Androcles:	*(whispering)* Did you see? A lion.

Megaera:	*(despairing)* The gods have sent him to punish us because you're a Christian. Take me away, Andy. Save me.
Androcles:	*(rising)* Meggy: there's one chance for you. It'll take him pretty nigh twenty minutes to eat me (I'm rather stringy and tough) and you can escape in less time than that.
Megaera:	Oh, don't talk about eating. *(The lion rises with a great groan and limps towards them.)* Oh! *(She faints.)*

2. Select one of the preceding scenes or the scene from *A Young Lady of Property* on page 113. Conduct an in-depth examination of it and write an introduction. Practice your vocal and physical delivery; then interpret the dramatic literature for an audience. Unless your teacher tells you otherwise, memorize the scene for performance and present it in its entirety.

3. Prepare to perform a scene of your choice from dramatic literature. Work within a minimum of five minutes and a maximum of ten minutes, including the introduction. Go through all parts of the interpretation process as you analyze, rehearse, and prepare for performance. Then present your interpretation for an audience. ■

9 Group Interpretation

The More, the Merrier . . .

Have you ever played in a band, worked on a club project, or belonged to a group of any kind? If you have, you may know the joy of combining your talents with the skills of other people. Oral interpretation, too, provides opportunities to cooperate with others. When you perform with someone else, there is a kind of shared energy that adds to the excitement of the project and encourages new learning.

Reading Together

When oral interpreters combine their voices to bring to life a work of literature, their performance is called **choral reading** or **choral speaking.** The tradition of choral speaking dates back to early Greek drama when the members of the chorus spoke together. Today, we practice choral speaking on a variety of occasions. When you recite the Pledge of Allegiance in the classroom or at an assembly, for instance, you are blending your voice with the voices of others. Choral speaking is often a part of patriotic presentations. You will also find such speaking used at religious assemblies.

When oral interpreters combine their voices, each participant can read some lines separately as well as with the group, or several voices can combine to read different passages in unison. Usually the voices are put together to match vocal qualities as much as possible. For example, just as a singing choir groups sopranos, altos, tenors, and basses, choral readers can be grouped by timbre or vocal quality. In this way the words spoken will receive a special coloring depending on which individual or combined voices are reading them. However, any group arrangement is possible as long as the end result is a melodic and harmonious blending of voices.

Activity 1   Choral Speaking

1. Form a choral speaking team with eight to twelve other readers. One reader should also serve as the director. Divide the team into four subgroups reflecting vocal quality. Read "The Voice," a choral reading exercise designed by Gale Nelson. Have each team perform for the class. If possible, record the performances and then listen to them.

"THE VOICE"

Group 1:   The voice, have you heard it?
                  It's lovely and clear.

Group 2:   The voice, have you heard it?
                  It's cold and austere.

Group 3:   And sometimes it's mellow
                  With round, rhythmic hum.

Group 4:   And sometimes it's heavy,
                  With beat like a drum.

Group 1:   And once, I remember,
                  It murmured a word.

Group 2:   It whispered so softly
                  That nobody heard.

Group 3:   And once it cried loudly,
                  With anger it rang.

Group 4:   And once it moaned sadly,
                  With pathos it sang.

Group 1:   Oh, what an instrument.

Group 2:   Oh, what a tool!

Group 3:   The voice, quite amazing,

Group 4:   A treasure, a jewel.

2. For the purpose of experimentation, change the voices assigned to read each part. Read the selection aloud again. If possible, record this reading and listen to it to see how the shifts have affected the overall sound of the reading. ■

Creating the Ensemble Effect

Choral reading has always served as an opportunity for individuals to share with others in the interpretation process. It is a particularly good way for beginning performers to learn basic interpretation skills and for experienced interpreters to experiment with vocal technique. The key to successful choral speaking is a unified, coordinated ensemble effect. Each individual blends with other voices to create a sound. Each voice is equally important, and all voices in harmony make the reading connect with an audience.

Timing is another important element in the ensemble effect. Each reader needs to pay close attention and be ready to come in on cue so that the flow of the language in enhanced. If one voice comes in late or cuts off a sound too soon, the quality of the performance is lessened.

While many choral readings are taken from poetry, poems are not the only sources. For instance, the Preamble to the Constitution and the Gettysburg Address are excellent possibilities for choral speaking; and Martin Luther King's "I Have a Dream" speech can be arranged to make a powerful reading.

In preparing a choral reading, you need to study the literature just as you would when preparing an individual selection. First, you would need to know what's going on in the material: What do the words mean? What's taking place? Who's speaking? Is there someone listening? In a solo interpretation you have an individual persona. Here you have a collective persona: townspeople, patriotic citizens, or a community of storytellers. Your team will need to decide who its voices will represent, and that decision will dictate many of the other choices you make about the interpretation.

If you are working with poetry, examine the rhythm, sound harmonies, and imagery. Know how the structure and the content support one another. If you are working with prose, study the sentence structures, phrasing, language, and build. Do more than just read the words of the selection as a group; prepare to share your discoveries about the literature through an orchestrated vocal performance. Because choral reading places paramount emphasis on the voice, movement is generally quite limited.

You may need to write an introduction for the reading. Just as with an individual selection, the goal of the introduction is to prepare the audience members and excite their interest in and anticipation of the selection. The introduction could be presented by a single individual in the group or by the entire group.

Activity 2   Orchestrating a Selection

Following are several selections to use for choral speaking. Work in teams of six to twelve people. Within the teams, divide by vocal quality into three to four groups. After choosing one reading, study the selection with your team, write an introduction, and prepare to give a performance. For some selections, group division of lines is already suggested. The team may adjust the line assignments to better fit the group, if necessary. Practice and evaluate the work you are doing as a group before you perform for the class.

"ALONE"

by Maya Angelou

Group 1: Lying, thinking
Last night
How to find my soul a home
Where water is not thirsty
And bread loaf is not stone . . .

Group 2: I came up with one thing
And I don't believe I'm wrong
That nobody,
But nobody
Can make it out here alone.

Group 3: Alone, all alone
Nobody, but nobody
Can make it out here alone.

Group 1: There are some millionaires
With money they can't use . . .

Group 2: Their wives run round like banshees . . .

Group 3: Their children sing the blues.

Group 2: They've got expensive doctors
To cure their hearts of stone.

Group 3:	But nobody No nobody Can make it out here alone.
Group 1:	Alone, all alone Nobody, but nobody Can make it out here alone.
Group 3:	Now if you listen closely I'll tell you what I know . . .
Group 1:	Storm clouds are gathering . . .
Group 2:	The wind is gonna blow . . .
Group 3:	The race of man is suffering And I can hear the moan,
Group 1:	Cause nobody, But nobody Can make it out here alone.
Group 2:	All, all alone
Group 3:	Nobody, but nobody Can make it out here alone.

FROM THE GOOD EARTH
by Pearl Buck

Pearl Buck's novel tells the story of Chinese peasant Wang Lung, his wife, and the family they found that will one day become a dynasty. Of particular importance is his relationship with the land that sustains him and the land he makes prosper.

Group 1:	Wang Lung was working hard with the growing wheat. He worked with his hoe, day after day. His back throbbed with weariness.
Group 2:	One day, her shadow fell across the ground over which he bent himself. There she stood, with a hoe across her shoulder.
Girl Solo:	"There is nothing to do until nightfall,"
Group 4:	she said. Without speech, she took the piece of ground to the left of him. She fell into steady hoeing.
Group 3:	The sun beat down upon them, for it was early summer. Her face was soon dripping with sweat. Wang Lung had his coat off. His back was bare. But she worked with her thin coat covering her shoulders. It grew wet and clung to her like skin.
Group 2:	They moved in time with each other, hour after hour. They did not say a word. He felt close to her, and it took the pain from his labor. He did not think, in words, of anything. There was only movement, and turning this earth of theirs over and over to the sun.
Group 1:	The earth formed their home and fed their bodies.
Group 2:	The earth lay rich and dark.
Group 3:	It fell apart lightly under the points of their hoes.
Group 4:	Sometimes they turned up a bit of brick, a splinter of wood. It was nothing.
Group 3:	Some time, in some age, bodies of men and women had been buried there.

Group 1: Houses had stood there. They had fallen and gone back into the earth. So also would their house, some time, return into the earth. So would their bodies also. Each had his turn at this earth.

Group 2: They worked on, moving together. They were making this earth give fruit. They did not speak in their movement together.

Group 3: When the sun had set, he straightened his back slowly and looked at the woman. Her face was wet and streaked with the earth. She was as brown as the very soil itself. Her wet, dark clothes stuck to her square body.

Group 4: She smoothed a last patch of earth. Then in her usual plain way, she spoke, straight out. Her voice was flat and very plain in the silent evening air.

Girl Solo: "I am with child."

Group 1: Wang Lung stood still.

Group 2: What was there to say about this thing?

Group 3: She stopped to pick up a bit of broken brick.

Group 4: It was as though she had said,

Girl Solo: "I have brought you tea."

Group 1: Or as though she had said,

Girl Solo: "We can eat."

Group 2: It seemed as ordinary as that to her!

Group 3: But to him—he could not say what it was to him. His heart swelled. It stopped as though there was no room for it to beat.

Group 4: He took the hoe suddenly from her hand. Then he spoke, his voice thick in his throat.

Boy Solo: "Let be for now. It is a day's end."

"The Unicorn"

by L. D. Naegelin

Group 1: In Rainbow Forest by Melody Lake
Lived a beast with a single horn.
He was swift as the wind as he pranced and he danced,
This magical unicorn.

Group 2: But beyond the forest lived an evil knight
Who hunted both valley and hill.
And early one morning his party rode out
When the air was crisp with its chill.

Group 3: "Away, away, we gallop away,
Ride fast, ride hard, ride far.
We ride to capture the unicorn
By the light of the morning star."

Group 4: For if they could lasso the magical beast,
They would hold him in their power.
So to Rainbow Forest they made their way
While the dew still slept on the flower.

Group 1: "Come softly, ride slowly, don't make any noise.
We must strike with silent surprise.
Move into place, be ready to act,
For soon the sun will rise."

Group 2: The silver-white creature slept by a tree.
A crackle caused him to wake.
His startled eyes sparked and looked around.
He sensed evil at Melody Lake.

Group 3: "You must flee, you must fly,"

Group 4:   the wind seemed to cry.

Group 1: "The hunters come with their rope.
You must take to the marsh where the reeds grow tall,
To the marsh, it's your only hope."

Group 2: "Wait there till the golden eagle comes
To accompany you in flight.
He'll escort you to the mountains.
It's there you'll be safe until night."

Group 3: "Then when the dazzling stars come out,
Go eagerly on your way.
Approach the canyons of shimmering ice,
A comet will light the way."

Group 4: But before the unicorn could run,
The intruders did surround.
And a ring of rope swirled toward his neck.
It twirled with a swishing sound.

Group 1: "He's ours, he's ours! We hold him fast.
He cannot get away.
His magic will be ours to use,
We've captured him today."

Group 2: But with a tug the unicorn
Snapped the rope in two.
And swiftly toward the marshland,
He charged, he dashed, he flew.

Group 3: "Make haste, make haste to follow.
The chase will now begin.
We'll ride beyond the mountains.
We won't give up, give in."

Group 4: But the unicorn was swifter,
All nature was his friend.
He was guided by an eagle;
He was carried on the wind.

Group 1: And as the darkness claimed the day,
A comet lit the night.
And through the drifts of fallen snow,
The unicorn made his flight.

Group 2: The hunters tried to follow.
But they lost their way quite soon.
For the unicorn had journeyed
To the mountains of the moon.

Group 3: Now in the Rainbow Forest
The trees have all turned gray.

Group 4: The flowers are brown and wilted,
And only shadows play.

Group 1:	The evil knight sits sullen
	Beside the silent lake
Group 2:	Where sounds of joy have gone to sleep,
	Never to come awake.
Group 3:	The beauty of the country
	Has vanished in a day,
Group 4:	For the miraculous,
Group 1:	magnificent
Group 2:	unicorn,
Group 3:	Has taken his magic away.
Group 4:	He's taken
Group 2:	his magic.
Group 1:	away. ∎

Group and Duo Interpretation

Two other types of performances that involve more than a single interpreter are **group interpretation** and **duo interpretation**. Duo interpretation seems to be gaining popularity as a classroom activity. Although guidelines for group and duo interpretation are not consistent across the country, particularly in terms of contest performance, some common elements can provide direction for interpreters.

Group and duo interpretation selections, like those in interpretation of drama, are usually taken from a published source, most often a play. A group interpretation also may be taken from a fictional or nonfictional work or a poem. If the presentation is performed by a group, there will be three or more readers, usually not more than eight. Duo interpretation of course limits the number of performers to two.

In both group and duo interpretation, the performers usually work from scripts held in folders. When scripts are used, there should be a reasonable balance of eye contact with the script and with the audience. Gestures should be appropriate to the literature being presented and effective for characterization. Use of properties or costumes is usually forbidden in contest performance; in the classroom, however, such restriction need not exist, though props and costumes are not essential.

In group interpretation the ensemble members may choose to use onstage or offstage focus as they work to create a unified performance. Offstage focus is a bit more common. The diagrams illustrate the difference.

Offstage Focus

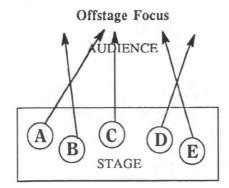

Onstage Focus

AUDIENCE

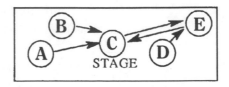

Getting Started in Oral Interpretation

Readers may stand or sit, and movement within the space being used for the interpretation is permitted, at times encouraged.

In contrast, in duo interpretation the readers almost always stand, usually turned away from each other at slight angles. They respond vocally and physically to each other's verbal and nonverbal cues while maintaining an offstage focus. Usually no movement around the performance area is allowed, but each performer may pivot or turn in his or her own stage location. At no time other than during the introduction or transitions do the performers look at one another, and they never touch.

Time limits vary, but they usually range between ten and fifteen minutes. Your teacher may adjust these times for your own class study. As with other performance events, effective introductions enhance both group and duo interpretations and are included, along with transitions, as part of the allocated time.

If the interpretation comes from a play, each reader usually portrays only one character, though both may share in the introduction and transitions. If the selection is prose or poetry, then, too, each reader generally plays only one character, but again all readers may share with introduction, transitions, and narration.

Guidelines for both these activities can be adapted to serve the needs of a class. The goal for performance should always be to share the literature effectively. To do that, honest characterizations are required, so the approach to analysis and performance will follow the steps outlined in Chapters 7 and 8. The major difference is that now a partner or several partners are sharing in the process. Now each performer embodies a character and finds motivation in that character's intentions. Rather than concentrating on pops as you move from character to character, you need to be certain that your character really listens to what is being said. In duo interpretation the performers may not be facing one another; nevertheless, they need to react to each other realistically and completely. The process of character study in these two activities is the same as in the interpretation of drama; it is the approach to presentation, the technique, that is different. And unlike acting, each performer in group and duo interpretation responds to specific verbal and nonverbal stimuli without being in a face-to-face situation.

Good performance means that all these elements work together to create a presentation in which vocal skill and physical control combine to create characters that will captivate the audience.

Activity 3   Putting It All Together

1. Here are several short scenes for duo or group interpretation. Depending on whether you choose to work with one other person or several, prepare the appropriate scene using the processes you have learned. You may also consider the scenes at the end of Chapter 8.

A YOUNG LADY OF PROPERTY
by Horton Foote

Characters: Wilma, Arabella

Set in the fictitious town of Harrison, Texas, Foote's play concerns Wilma Thompson, a fifteen-year-old girl whose dying mother left her the family house and property. The year is 1925, and Wilma, now living with her Aunt Gertrude, is attempting to come to terms with herself and her irresponsible father. Arabella Cookenboo is Wilma's best friend, her adoring shadow and slave. Believing that an escape to stardom might add excitement to their lives, both girls have written for a Hollywood screen test. Now that the responses have arrived, however, Arabella is having second thoughts.

Wilma: Heh, Arabella. Come sit and swing.

Arabella: All right. Your letter came.

Wilma: Whoopie. Where is it?

Arabella: Here. *(She gives it to her.* Wilma *tears it open. She reads.)*

Wilma: *(Reading)* Dear Miss Thompson: Mr. Delafonte will be glad to see you any time next week about your contemplated screen test. We suggest you call the office when you arrive in the city and we will set an exact time. Yours truly, Adele Murray. Well . . . Did you get yours?

Arabella: Yes.

Wilma: What did it say?

Arabella: The same.

Wilma: Exactly the same?

Arabella: Yes.

Wilma: Well, let's pack our bags. Hollywood, here we come.

Arabella: Wilma . . .

Wilma: Yes?

Arabella: I have to tell you something . . . Well . . . I . . .

Wilma: What is it?

Arabella: Well . . . promise me you won't hate me, or stop being my friend. I never had a friend, Wilma, until you began being nice to me, and I couldn't stand it if you weren't my friend any longer . . .

Wilma: Oh, my cow. Stop talking like that. I'll never stop being your friend. What do you want to tell me?

Arabella: Well . . . I don't want to go to see Mr. Delafonte, Wilma . . .

Wilma: You don't?

Arabella: No. I don't want to be a movie star. I don't want to leave Harrison or my mother or father . . . I just want to stay here the rest of my life and get married and settle down and have children.

Wilma: Arabella . . .

Arabella: I just pretended like I wanted to go to Hollywood because I knew you wanted me to, and I wanted you to like me . . .

Wilma: Oh, Arabella . . .

Arabella: Don't hate me, Wilma. You see, I'd be afraid . . . I'd die if I had to go to see Mr. Delafonte. Why, I even get faint when I have to recite before the class. I'm not like you. You're not scared of anything.

Wilma: Why do you say that?

Arabella: Because you're not. I know.

Wilma: Oh, yes, I am. I'm scared of lots of things.

Arabella: What?

Wilma: Getting lost in a city. Being bitten by dogs. Old lady Leighton taking my daddy away . . . *(A pause.)*

Arabella: Will you still be my friend?

Wilma: Sure. I'll always be your friend.

Arabella: I'm glad. Oh, I almost forgot. Your Aunt Gert said for you to come on home.

Wilma: I'll go in a little. I love to swing in my front yard. Aunt Gert has a swing in her front yard, but it's not the same. Mama and I used to come out here and swing together. Some nights when Daddy was out all night gambling, I used to wake up and hear her out here swinging away. Sometimes she'd let me come and sit beside her. We'd swing until three or four in the morning. *(A pause. She looks out into the yard.)* The pear tree looks sickly, doesn't it? The fig trees are doing nicely though. I was out in back and the weeds are near knee high, but fig trees just seem to thrive in the weeds. The freeze must have killed off the banana trees . . . *(A pause. Wilma stops swinging—she walks around the yard.)* Maybe I won't leave either. Maybe I won't go to Hollywood after all.

Arabella: You won't?

Wilma: No. Maybe I shouldn't. That just comes to me now. You know sometimes my old house looks so lonesome it tears at my heart. I used to think it looks lonesome just whenever it had no tenants, but now it comes to me it has looked lonesome ever since Mama died and we moved away, and it will look lonesome until some of us move back here. Of course, Mama can't, and Daddy won't. So it's up to me.

Arabella: Are you gonna live here all by yourself?

Wilma: No. I talk big about living here by myself, but I'm too much of a coward to do that. But maybe I'll finish school and live with Aunt Gert and keep on renting the house until I meet some nice boy with good habits and steady ways, and marry him. Then we'll move here and have children and I bet this old house won't be lonely any more. I'll get Mama's old croquet set and put it out under the pecan trees and play croquet with the children, or sit in this yard and swing and wave to people as they pass by.

Arabella: Oh, I wish you would. Mama says that's a normal life for a girl, marrying and having children. She says being an actress is all right, but the other's better.

Wilma: Maybe I've come to agree with your mama. Maybe I was going to Hollywood out of pure lonesomeness. I felt so alone with Mrs. Leighton getting my daddy and my mama having left the world. Daddy could have taken away my lonesomeness, but he didn't want to or couldn't. Aunt Gert says nobody is lonesome with a house full of children, so maybe that's what I just ought to stay here and have . . .

Arabella: Have you decided on a husband yet?

Wilma: No.

Arabella: Mama says that's the bad feature of being a girl, you have to wait for the boy to ask you and just pray that the one you want wants you. Tommy Murray is nice, isn't he?

Wilma: I think so.

Arabella: Jay Godfrey told me once he wanted to ask you for a date, but he didn't dare because he was afraid you'd turn him down.

Wilma: Why did he think that?

Arabella: He said the way you talked he didn't think you would go out with anything less than a movie star.

Wilma:	Maybe you'd tell him different . . .
Arabella:	All right. I think Jay Godfrey is very nice. Don't you?
Wilma:	Yes, I think he's very nice and Tommy is nice . . .
Arabella:	Maybe we could double-date sometimes.
Wilma:	That might be fun.
Arabella:	Oh, Wilma. Don't go to Hollywood. Stay here in Harrison and let's be friends forever . . .
Wilma:	All right. I will.
Arabella:	You will?
Wilma:	Sure, why not? I'll stay here. I'll stay and marry and live in my house.

FROM THE CRUCIBLE
by Arthur Miller

Characters: Abigail, Mercy, Mary, Betty

Set in Salem, Massachusetts, in 1692, Miller's play deals with the Salem witch trials. A young girl named Abigail becomes the catalyst for the hysteria that develops. Wild and undisciplined, she will do whatever is necessary to protect herself and get what she wants. Her great desire is to win John Proctor away from his wife.

In an early scene in the play, Abigail and several of the other village girls come together in the home of Reverend Parris. They have been caught dancing in the woods. Betty fainted from fear and is now in bed. It is now in her room that Abby plots to insure their safety in an atmosphere alive with the talk of witchcraft.

Abigail:	*(With hushed trepidation)* How is Ruth sick?
Mercy:	It's weirdish, I know not—she seems to walk like a dead one since last night.
Abigail:	*(Turns at once and goes to Betty, and now, with fear in her voice)* Betty? *(Betty doesn't move. She shakes her.)* Now stop this! Betty! Sit up now! *(Betty doesn't stir. Mercy comes over.)*
Mercy:	Have you tried beatin' her? I gave Ruth a good one and it waked her for a minute. Here, let me have her.
Abigail:	*(Holding Mercy back)* No, he'll be comin' up. Listen, now; if they be questioning us, tell them we danced—I told him as much already.
Mercy:	Aye. And what more?
Abigail:	He knows Tituba conjured Ruth's sister to come out of the grave.
Mercy:	And what more? . . . . *(Enter Mary Warren, breathless. She is seventeen, a subservient, naive, lonely girl.)*
Mary:	What'll we do? The village is out! I just come from the farm; the whole country's talkin' witchcraft! They'll be callin' us witches, Abby!
Mercy:	*(Pointing and looking at Mary Warren)* She means to tell, I know it.
Mary:	Abby, we've got to tell. Witchery's a hangin' error, a hangin' like they done in Boston two year ago! We must tell the truth, Abby! You'll only be whipped for dancin', and the other things.
Abigail:	Oh, *we'll* be whipped!

Mary:	I never done none of it, Abby. I only looked!
Mercy:	*(Moving menacingly toward Mary)* Oh, you're a great one for lookin' aren't you, Mary Warren? What a grand peeping courage you have!
	(Betty, on the bed, whimpers. Abigail turns to her at once.)
Abigail:	Betty? *(She goes to Betty.)* Now, Betty, dear, wake up now. It's Abigail. *(She furiously shakes her.)* I'll beat you, Betty! *(Betty whimpers.)* My, you seem improving. I talked to your papa and I told him everything. So there's nothing to—
Betty:	*(Darts off bed, frightened of Abigail, and flattens herself against the wall.)* I want my mama!
Abigail:	*(With alarm, as she cautiously approaches Betty.)* What ails you, Betty? Your mama's dead and buried.
Betty:	I'll fly to Mama. Let me fly! *(She raises her arms as though to fly and streaks for the window.)*
Abigail:	*(Pulling her away from the window)* I told him everything; he knows now, he knows everything we—
Betty:	You drank blood, Abby! You didn't tell him that!
Abigail:	Betty, you never say that again! You will never—
Betty:	You did, you did! You drank a charm to kill John Proctor's wife! You drank a charm to kill Goody Proctor!
Abigail:	*(Smashes her across the face)* Shut it! Now shut it!
Betty:	*(Collapsing)* Mama! Mama! *(She dissolves into sobs.)*
Abigail:	Now look you. All of you. We danced. And Tituba conjured Ruth Putnam's dead sisters. And that is all. And mark this. Let either of you breathe a word, or the edge of a word, about the other things, and I will come to you in the black of some terrible night and I will bring a pointy reckoning that will shudder you. And you know I can do it; I saw Indians smash my dear parents' heads on the pillow next to mine, and I have seen some reddish work done at night, and I can make you wish you had never seen the sun go down! *(She goes to Betty.)* Now you—sit up and stop this! *(Betty collapses.)*
Mary:	*(With hysterical fright)* What's got her? *(Abigail stares in fright at Betty.)* Abby, she's going to die! It's a sin to conjure, and we—
Abigail:	*(Starting for Mary)* I say shut it, Mary Warren!

FROM BIG RIVER
by William Hauptman,
Adapted from *Huckleberry Finn* by Mark Twain

Characters: Huck, Tom, Ben, Jo, Simon

William Hauptman's script for his musical follows Huckleberry Finn from the Widow Douglas' house, down the Mississippi with Jim, through his adventures with the King and the Duke, to the Phelps farm. Scene two in the play involves Huck, Tom, and a group of friends meeting at Injun Joe's Cave to establish a gang of robbers and killers.

| Huck: | *(To audience)* That night, instead of sleeping, I shinnied down the drainpipe and got clean away from the Widow Douglas and Miss Watson. It was a lonesome night . . . . *(A hooting sound. Huck grins and hoots in reply.)* Tom Sawyer! Is that you? |

Tom: Come along, Huck!

Huck: Where we going?

Tom: Injun Joe's Cave!

Huck: *(To audience)* So I followed him, through the graveyard and down to the river. Then we took the towpath until we came to the big scar on the hillside and there we crawled through a hole and into the cave, whose walls was all of clay—damp, sweaty, and cold as a corpse.

Tom: Now we're going to start this gang of robbers and call it Tom Sawyer's Gang.

Ben: What's the line of business of this gang?

Tom: Nothing, only robbery and murder.

Ben: Bully.

Tom: Whoever wants to join has got to take this oath, and sign his name in blood.

Jo: What's it say, Tom?

Tom: It swears every boy to stick to the gang, and never tell any of its secrets. And if he does, he must have his throat cut, then have his carcass burnt up and the ashes scattered around, and his name blotted off the list, and never mentioned by the gang but have a curse put on it and be forgot forever.

Ben: Real beautiful, Tom!

Simon: You get that out of your own head?

Tom: *(Modestly)* Some. The rest is out of pirate and robber books.

Ben: Be a good idea to kill the families of the boys who tell the secrets too.

Tom: I'll write it in.

Jo: But here's Huck Finn—he ain't got a family.

Simon: Then we got to rule him out.

Ben: Yeah, every boy's got to have a family or somebody to kill, or it wouldn't be fair and square for the others.

Huck: *(To audience)* I almost cried when I though they weren't going to allow me in Tom Sawyer's gang, but just then I got an idea. *(To boys)* There's Miss Watson, the lady who's taking care of me—you can kill her.

Ben: Bully.

Tom: There you go; she'll do. Huck can come in. Now—everybody stick their finger with this knife to get some blood, and we'll seal the oath.

(They prick their fingers and pass the oath around.) . . .

Ben: Who we going to rob? Houses? Or cattle? Or people?

Tom: That ain't no sort of style! We are highwaymen. We stop stages and kill the people and steal their watches and money.

. . .

Simon: Do we always kill the people?

Tom: Oh, certainly. It's best. Some authorities think different, but mostly it's considered best just to kill them.

Jo: Do we kill the women too?

Tom: Jo Harper, if I was as ignorant as you, I wouldn't let on! Kill the women? No—you fetch 'em to the cave, and you're always as polite as pie to 'em;

and by and by, they fall in love with you and never want to go home anymore.

Jo: Well, if that's the way, then I'm agreed.

Tom: Good . . . . Everybody signed?

Jo: *(Trying to prick his finger with knife)* Ouch.

Ben: You big crybaby.

Jo: Am not.

Ben: Are so.

Jo: Am not.

Ben: Are so.

Jo: You call me a crybaby, I'm going to tell everybody the secrets.

Tom: Hold on! No fighting amongst club members. *(Gives Jo a nickel.)*

Jo: But . . .

Tom: Here's a nickel; now keep your trap shut.

Simon: Tom, I got to be going home anyway.

Tom: All right, go home—then we'll get together next week and rob some people and kill some people.

Ben: I can only get out on Sundays. Let's begin on Sunday.

Jo: It'd be wicked to do it on Sunday.

Ben: Great big sissy.

Jo: Am not.

Ben: Are so!

Tom: *(Averting an argument)* Let's just agree to get together and fix a date soon as possible.

Ben: So long, Tom, Huck.

Tom: They don't seem to know nothing, somehow, do they?—perfect sapheads.

Huck: . . . What are we going to do with all our money, Tom?

Tom: I don't know, Huck. Just think of it: six thousand dollars apiece—all gold—found right here in this cave. . . . What *are* we going to do with it?

Huck: Light out for the western territories.

Tom: Thunderation!

Huck: That's what I been thinking.

Tom: It's a capital idea! I'll go with you!

Huck: Will you?

Tom: Just as soon as this year of school is out. . . . Say, it's getting late, we'd better be going. *(Socks Huck on the arm.)*

Huck: *(To audience)* But I knowed Tom Sawyer didn't mean it, no more than he meant all that talk about robbing and killing. And if he wouldn't go with me, who would?

2. Teaming with one other person or with a group of people, find a novel, short story, or play that you would like to perform as a duo interpretation or a group interpretation. Prepare a cutting that will run between eight and twelve minutes including the introduction. Be certain that everyone involved has some part to play. Studying and rehearsing the scene, cut in order to prepare the literature for presentation to an audience. After cutting and rehearsing the scene, present it to an audience. ■

10 Rehearsal and Evaluation

Get Ready . . . Get Better . . . Go!

When you hear the word *rehearsal,* what flashes through your mind? Perhaps you think of *times* people practice, as for a play, a piano recital, a wedding, a variety show, or a soccer game. Instead of thinking of times, maybe you picture the work involved, the methodical preparation that goes into getting ready to perform. Learning to play an instrument or master some other skill, for instance, takes time, effort, and concentration. The process is demanding and can be painstaking.

Then, throughout the time you practice and continuing even after the game is played or the concert performed, numerous assessments of progress and outcome provide feedback—everything from "Don't rush the notes!" to "You ran a perfect pattern to score the goal!" Evaluation is an integral part of the learning process, for it examines strengths and weaknesses, high points and areas needing improvement.

Both rehearsal and evaluation are equally essential. Without consistent, planned practice and meaningful assessment of yourself as well as others, your growth as a performer will be limited.

Rehearsing as Part of the Overall Process

The practice period before a performance includes all the work you do to prepare your selection to be shared with an audience, everything from familiarizing yourself with the script to memorizing each word, if memorization is required; everything from developing characters imaginatively to performing them physically.

Evaluating your growth as you rehearse can often be more beneficial than evaluating your performance. From the beginning it's important to understand that rehearsal is serious business. Therefore, it is imperative that you evaluate how seriously you approach your work. Following are three questions you should ask yourself.

Do I have a specific goal for my rehearsal?

An early goal might be just to familiarize yourself with the selection. This task can be accomplished by reading through the literature several times to get comfortable with the words and the flow of the sentences. Another rehearsal might be devoted to characterization. The goal here could be to develop a dialect or chart the subtext. Still other rehearsals might be devoted to the goal of memorization, the goal of perfecting transitions, or the goal of playing character intentions.

Am I following my plan, and have I allocated sufficient time to accomplish the goal?

Depending on what you want to accomplish during a particular rehearsal, your approach will be different. If your goal is to memorize, for instance, you must decide how much of the selection you wish to memorize during the rehearsal and then allow adequate time to achieve the desired outcome. If you are refining characterization, you may choose to rehearse just one area of the selection that is proving to be difficult. The entire practice session may be devoted to going over that one area again and again until you have eliminated your problem. If you are polishing the entire performance, however, you will need to run through the complete selection. You may wish to videotape it so that you can see what you are doing, or make an audiotape of your rehearsal. Perhaps you will want another student to watch and give you feedback.

Are my rehearsal techniques working?

Unless you ask yourself this important question and arrive at a clear answer, you'll never know to what extent practicing is paying off. One good way to keep track of progress is to keep a written record of your rehearsal accomplishments. That way those techniques that are really proving beneficial will become obvious, and you'll know to rely on them in the future. The written record can be shared with your teacher or classmates to indicate what you wanted to achieve and how well you feel you are meeting your personal goals.

Because the rehearsal process should be planned and should provide a variety of approaches to help you improve your work, you might want to try some of the following rehearsal techniques:

• Spend a day as a character.

From the time you get out of bed in the morning until you go to bed at night, do everything as your character would. If an entire day in character is impractical, then try, for example, a Saturday afternoon. Go shopping as your character; eat as your character; visit with friends as your character; play tennis as your character. The more time you can spend in your characters' bodies, the more you will make them real for yourself and your audience.

• Play the "In Other Words" game.

If you are having trouble getting across the meaning of a particular line or lines, use your own words instead of the author's to say the same thing. Perhaps work with a partner who, when your line-delivery of the written script becomes unconvincing, calls out "in other words." That's your cue to paraphrase, to put the idea in your own words until you get the right feeling. Then go back to the author's exact words.

• Improvise scenes with your characters.

Put the characters in very different or very similar situations and see what happens as they respond. This activity can also be done with a partner, who can play the other role(s) in the scene.

- Act out your interpretation as you would in a play.

The dramatic motions you go through will provide the basis for the muscle memory you need to call on later. Again, you may do this exercise alone or with a partner.

- Work on portions of the literature other than your excerpt to give you additional insight.

This technique can be particularly helpful if a selection is losing its excitement or spontaneity for you.

- Play the scene without saying words.

This technique will force the face and body to carry the message. Whether you work with a partner or alone, this activity is great for building concentration.

- Imagine yourself going through the selection and performing it perfectly.

Such positive imaging produces positive results. You may also daydream and imagine your characters in a movie. What you envision can give you ideas for your characterizations.

- Speak the lines in very different ways than you have been.

Try whispering them, or shouting them; try speeding them up or slowing them down. The new way of saying lines often helps you discover new meanings.

- Devote a rehearsal to speaking only the subtext.

Then you can see how the characters are relating to each other beneath the lines. This activity is difficult, but it really helps you to think as the characters are thinking and get the complexity of the characters.

Activity 1   Working with Rehearsal Techniques

1. As you prepare for an oral performance, make use of at least three of the rehearsal techniques suggested. Be certain that you answer the three questions on page 121 as you evaluate your rehearsal work.
2. Keep a written record assessing your rehearsal progress. The important point is not the amount you write, but the specific detail you record in identifying goals and plans and appraising personal growth.
3. Of the different rehearsal techniques you tried, which one was the most useful? Why do you think it helped you the most?
4. Develop your own exercises to eliminate problems in rehearsal that you or your class-mates have experienced as beginning performers of literature. ■

Evaluating Your Own Performance

Just as you evaluate your progress during the rehearsal process, you also need to evaluate each performance, whether given for a class, an invited audience, or a set of contestants and judges at a tournament. True, you may get a written evaluation from a critic who observes your interpretation, but equally important is your personal assessment of what you have accomplished though your performance. Questions that might assist you in your personal assessment include:

- Did my introduction allow me to present myself and connect with my audience?

Usually, a performer can feel whether or not his or her introduction *connected*. Perhaps some audience members responded more openly than others. Maybe someone in the audience seemed turned off by the introduction. Going through a quick assessment can assist you in determining whether or not you may want to change your introduction before another presentation. Such assessment can certainly guide you in constructing introductions for other literature.

- Was my characterization consistent and honest throughout the performance?

Perhaps you presented a first-person prose interpretation or a monologue. If so, assess how completely you created that one character and how evenly you maintained that characterization. If your selection had multiple characters, then evaluate how successfully you breathed life into each one. You also need to consider whether or not you maintained each character as an independent entity throughout the performance. A common error of oral interpreters is to allow one character to fall into the rhythm of another. All people have different physical rhythms, even when angry, and differentiation of rhythm is necessary for effective characterization. Being so in control of your characters that each one is totally believable is one way of knowing your interpretation has been successful.

- How effective was my vocal performance?

You want to be certain that you projected sufficiently and articulated clearly, that you convincingly created your character voices, and that you varied your tone and tempo to show motivation and convey action. You may have considered some of these vocal elements when you looked at overall characterization, but here you want to focus on specific vocal quality in creating nuances—subtle variations.

- How effective was my physical performance?

Evaluate your success in being spontaneous and responsive to the demands of the literature you performed. Did your gestures and movement flow naturally from the demands of the selection? Were you relaxed and spontaneous? Just as vocalization may overlap somewhat with characterization, so too does physicalization. For a moment, though, think just about how your body functioned in helping you create the interpretation. Identify moments when you felt you were truly reaching your audience as a result of your physicalization. Was there any moment when you sensed your body got in the way of your communication?

- Did I build the selection effectively and convey the meaning precisely?

Consider how effective you were in developing the progression of the selection from the opening action through the climax and denouement—the final outcome. Was the audience caught up in the build? Could you tell that everyone seemed to comprehend what was happening in the literary selection or did some members of the audience seem lost or confused? Being aware of how the audience is following the literature itself is important, especially if you have prepared a cutting or adaptation of a longer work. If you become aware that the audience was "lost" at a certain point in the performance, you may be able to re-edit or design a transition that can eliminate the problem next time.

- Did I feel good about the overall quality of my performance from beginning to end?

It's important to know exactly what sensation gripped you when you completed your performance. Were you pleased with everything you did? Truth is that if you are in an oral interpretation contest, a judge may disagree with what you do in your performance. If you are performing for an audience, not everyone may respond exactly as you might hope.

Nevertheless, if you judge that your performance met your personal standards and satisfied you, then your performance was a success. Giving yourself credit for successful performances is an essential part of becoming a good interpreter.

In your notebook you might sketch out a quick personal evaluation focusing on the preceding six questions or you might use a personal evaluation form such as the one on page 125. Remember, writing down your personal critique is essential to learning and growing. If you don't record your assessment of each performance while it is fresh in your mind, you won't remember what succeeded and what didn't. Furthermore, you won't have a written record to study as part of your long-term growth as an oral interpreter.

Some performers might argue that when they become totally involved in a performance, they are completely unaware of the audience. Therefore, it is impossible to assess every part of the performance. The more polished you become, the more possible this complete immersion into performance becomes. And it is perhaps this absolute concentration that every performer should work toward. Even when that happens, however, part of you is aware of your relationship with your audience, and you can evaluate what you accomplished. You may have only an overall impression, but even that impression is an evaluation worth recording.

If you react honestly and keep good notes, you will know what elements of your performance are peaking and which need improving. You might also discover that your selection connects better with certain types of audiences. For instance, one young man performing a selection about a boy and his Little League baseball coach from Pat Conroy's novel *The Great Santini* began to notice that, although the adolescents in his audiences responded positively as they listened to the selection, the adult judges at a contest seemed indifferent, and their rankings of his performance were mediocre. Interestingly enough, these judges generally wrote positive comments and made no reference to the selection's lack of appeal for them. It was not specific commentary from these judges, then, but the performer's assessment of their reactions during the performance that led him to re-edit the literature to give it wider appeal and ultimately bring him greater success.

Activity 2 Experimenting with Evaluation

1. Using a copy of the "Personal Evaluation Form" on page 125 or one you or your teacher has designed, evaluate one of your own oral interpretation performances.

2. Be prepared to discuss your assessment with your teacher or with students in your class. It would be extremely helpful if the individuals to whom you explain your personal evaluation could have heard your performance and critiqued it using the "Performance Evaluator's Comment Sheet" on page 127.

Becoming an Effective Critic

A **critic** is a person who renders some kind of verdict about a work, whether that work be a painting, a book, a theatrical production, or an individual oral interpretation performance. An effective critic, though, is more than a fault-finder. He or she goes beyond merely proclaiming a surface opinion; critics provide valid reasons or criteria justifying and explaining the judgment. These reasons should relate to specific inquiries about the literature being performed: "Are the characterizations consistent with what the literature suggests?" for example. At the same time, the criteria should relate to the elements of the performance: "Do the bodily actions flow smoothly and naturally?" And finally, criteria should be given proportionate value. For instance, creating a consistent vocal characterization is proportionally

Personal Evaluation Form

Name _____

Date of Performance _____ Place of Performance _____

Occasion of Performance _____

Title of Selection _____

Assessment of Introduction

    1. Was my delivery personal and conversational?

    2. Did I sense I connected with my audience? How do I know?

Characterization

    1. What was the greatest strength in my characterization work in this performance?

    2. What could I have done to strengthen my characterization work in this performance?

Vocal Performance

    1. Was there any element of my vocal performance that seemed to affect my audience?

    2. Was there anything about my vocal performance I would have changed?

Physical Performance

    1. Was there any element of my physical performance that seemed to excite my audience?

    2. Was there anything about my physical performance I would have changed?

Communication of Meaning

    What did I sense in the audience that made me feel they were actively involved in and understood the selection?

Overall Assessment

    1. What about my presentation made me feel most satisfied during this performance?

    2. What could have enhanced my performance?

more significant than a single slip in articulation. Likewise, one sloppy pop is proportionally less detracting from an overall performance than a total lapse in concentration or a break in character.

As a critical listener and performance evaluator, you must learn how to substantiate your judgments clearly and specifically. Imagine you have just given a performance after which you receive a comment sheet reading, "Good work, but gestures could be even better." Unless you know what specific qualities enhanced the performance to make it good and what prevented specific gestures from being effective, you will have no idea where you succeeded or how you might improve your work. Just as you deserve specific, quality comments, you must learn to give quality comments. That is especially important when you play the role of peer evaluator in the classroom.

One way to help yourself become an effective critic is to learn to ask and then answer the right questions. For instance, if you are evaluating an introduction, what should you look for? Does it contain required information—title and author, for instance? Does it draw you into the selection and prepare you for what is to come? Is the introduction presented in a natural, conversational way that allows the performer to introduce himself or herself? Is the introduction overly presentational, calling attention to itself more than introducing the performance?

The "Performance Evaluator's Comment Sheet" on page 127 sets up general areas a critic might evaluate. It even suggests a general set of questions to consider. But you, as you grow as an interpreter, will learn to make assessments based on your own knowledge and understanding of oral interpretation.

Demand of yourself to provide meaningful reasons to verify the judgements you make. If a poetry program doesn't seem to flow together the way it's constructed, tell the performer what is ineffective and suggest a reason for the failure. Perhaps the second poem throws the focus off the program theme because it doesn't communicate the message the interpreter assumes it does. Perhaps a better connecting transition could fix the problem, or maybe the performer could enhance the program by finding a better second poem.

If the performer is creating the character of Eliza Doolittle from Bernard Shaw's play *Pygmalion* with an Americanized accent rather than in the Cockney dialect, then you, as a critic, can explain that the character is inconsistent with the literature. Because the play deals with British class and manners, the correct dialect is essential to the scene.

Activity 3   Becoming a Conscientious Critic

1. Using copies of the "Performance Evaluator's Comment Sheet" or evaluation forms provided by your teacher, evaluate a minimum of three different oral interpretation performances, at least one of which is performed by an individual in your class.

2. Examine each of the comment sheets you have completed and decide which one is the most effective in terms of offering a clear, helpful, and substantiated critique.

3. Speak with the person in your class whom you evaluated and discuss your evaluation of his or her performance. Ask that person to assess the value of your critique.

4. If you have equipment available, have someone videotape one of your own performances. First, evaluate the presentation from your perspective as performer a immediately after your performance. Write the evaluation in your notebook or use the "Personal Evaluation Form." Now watch your taped performance with a classmate. Each of you should evaluate the taped performance as a critic and record your evaluation. Compare and discuss your

Performance Evaluator's Comment Sheet

Name of Performer _____

Name of Evaluator _____

Title of Selection _____

Comment on each of the areas below. Give specific reasons to support all evaluative judgments.

Introduction/Transitions [Is the introduction informational, relevant, enticing in content, and conversational in delivery; if there is transitional material, is it purposeful and appropriate?]

Insight and Understanding [Does the performer sense and then convey the literature's meaning; are relationships clear; is there appropriate build?]

Characterization [Does the performer capture the full nature of the narrator, persona, character, or characters and bring each to life believably; is each distinct?]

Vocal Control [Does the performer project and articulate? Are the characters' voices distinct and consistent? Does the performer vary tone and tempo appropriately and make good use of the pause? If the performance is poetry, does he or she control the rhythm and play the harmonies?]

Physicalization [Is the performer's body appropriately responsive to the demands of the literature being presented; are the movements definite, appropriate, and economical?]

Overall Effect [in terms of the total selection, were you carried into the literature completely and honestly; did the performer demonstrate good technique and appear well-rehearsed and polished?]

comments with your partner. Then look at your personal evaluation. Decide how each of these evaluations can enhance your performance skills. ■

A Final Word

From the time you begin preparing your interpretation until you perform it for the final time, you need to be concerned about evaluating your progress. To be certain that your rehearsals are a valuable part of the preparation process, learn to assess them. Use a variety of rehearsal techniques; through your evaluation process, determine which of these techniques prove most helpful to you.

As you perform, evaluate your presentations. As much as is possible without losing concentration, determine what is succeeding and what is not. Keep a record of your assessments to assist you in your growth. Likewise, learn to be an effective critic so that you can evaluate meaningfully the work of others. Quality evaluations do more than merely arrive at a verdict; they give substantiated reasons that serve to validate the judgments.

The strongest performers are those who master evaluation as part of the overall performance process. These individuals are also best prepared to make the kinds of judgments all creative thinkers have to make, whether they are performing the art of oral interpretation or just participating in the art of living successfully. Good luck as you learn to do both!

Glossary of Key Terms

analysis	a careful, studied exploration; also the process through which such an exploration into a work of literature takes place
articulation	the process of using hard and soft palates, lips, tongue and teeth to shape sound into clear words
build	the creation of a sense of growth and/or development by a performer as he or she presents a particular sequence or progresses from inciting incident to climax
caricature	the deliberate exaggeration or distortion of characters to produce a satiric effect
choral reading/speaking	the combination of voices by performers reading together to give a kind of musical quality to the presentation
comic sense	the ability of a performer to stress and/or time the delivery of a line in such a way that it produces laughter in the audience
commitment	the involvement of a performer totally and energetically in his or her actions
controlled relaxation	the happy balance between relaxation and energy necessary for performance
direct discourse	a word-for-word statement by a character, e.g., JOHN SAID, "I WILL GO."
duo interpretation	the performance of literature, especially drama, in which two interpreters equally share in the performance
dynamic character	a literary character who grows and develops as a person as a result of what happens to him or her
embody	to give body to; to allow the narrator, persona, or character to "take over" the performer's body so that the character rather than the performer appears to stand before the audience
empathic response	a performer's sense of feeling physically and emotionally with his or her characters; an audience's similar sense of feeling with a performer
evaluation	the process of assessing the positive and negative aspects of a performance
flat character	a simple, undeveloped character who is not totally fleshed-out by the author
focal point	the place or spot to which a performer looks to indicate the location of the "listening character" as seen by the "speaking character"
gesture	a general term used to refer to any movement of the body to convey an idea, including change in tension, adjustment of posture, or some specific movement of hands or arms
group interpretation	the performance of literature, especially drama, in which at least three or more interpreters are involved
indirect discourse	a reported statement of what a character said, e.g., JOHN SAID THAT HE WOULD GO.

intention	a specific goal toward which a character works
irony	a term describing the contrast between what appears to be and what really is; may be verbal—a contrast in literal meaning of what is said, situational—a contrast in the expected and intended meaning of an occurrence, or dramatic—a disparity of knowledge about a situation between characters or between a character and the audience or reader
mannerism	a specific action which a person habitually does so that the action characterizes the individual
master gesture	a specific gesture peculiar to a character and used by a performer to establish that character in the eyes of the audience
narrator	the speaker in a work of prose fiction
offstage focus	directing the energy to a spot "out front" or beyond the audience rather than to other characters on the stage
onstage focus	characters looking at and reacting face to face as on a stage during a play
oral interpretation	a specialized way of studying literature by performing it
pantomime	the use of physical actions to imitate business carried out in real life, e.g., the pretended pouring of a cup of coffee
persona	the implied speaker in a poem
pitch	a term used to denote the highness or lowness of vocal sound in comparison to a musical scale
poet-centered program	a poetry presentation consisting of several poems by one poet and focusing on some element of his or her style, some common thread, or different aspects of poet's career/development
point of view	the perspective or "eyes" through which a work of literature is told or presented
pop	a term used to denote the quick shift or transition from one speaking character to another during the oral performance of a literary work, especially drama
rate	a term used to denote the tempo or speed of speaking
rehearsal	the process of preparing for performance, including analyzing/studying the literature, memorizing the script—if required, working on characterization, practicing the performance, perfecting and polishing the elements of performance, and reworking the performance based on evaluations of it
rounded character	a fully developed character, one completely fleshed-out and three dimensional
scoring	the marking of a typed performance script in a way to indicate tempo shifts, pauses, and words, phrases, or ideas requiring special emphasis or coloring
static character	a literary character who remains unchanged despite what happens to him or her
subtext	an indication of what is happening under the lines of the script; what is going on inside a character's mind
theme-centered program	a poetry presentation consisting of several poems that focus on the same theme
unreliable narrator	a storyteller who has a distorted view of himself or herself or of other characters and whose account, therefore, may not be totally trusted
vocal quality	a particular attribute or coloring of a voice that makes it distinguishable from all others
volume	a term used to denote the quantity of sound; the loudness or softness of speech

Index of Literary Selections and Authors

Acosta, Teresa Palomo, 71-72
Adventures of Huckleberry Finn, The, 23, 27
"Ah, Are You Digging on my Grave?", 67
Alone, 108-9
Androcles and the Lion, 103-5
Angelou, Maya, 44-45, 108-9
Arithmetic, 53, 60
Aston, Jere, 50
Auto Wreck, 61-65
Betts, Doris, 24
Big River, 117-19
Borland, Hal, 45-46
Browning, Robert, 60, 70-71
Buck, Pearl, 109-10
Capote, Truman, 20
Cask of Amontillado, The, 29-39
Christmas Memory, A, 20
Coatsworth, Elizabeth, 51-52
Conroy, Pat, 42-44
Creation, The, 15
Crucible, The, 116-17
Dean, William, 50
Deer Hunt, 52-53, 60, 65
Defenseless Creature, A, 76-86, 91, 94-95
Dino, 82, 99-100
Fall of the House of Usher, The, 19
Foote, Horton, 113-16
Freddy, 54
Frost, Robert, 60, 69
Gilbert and Sullivan, 16
Good Earth, The, 109-10

Great Figure, The, 57-58
Great Santini, The, 42-44
Hardy, Thomas, 67
Hauptman, William, 117-19
Howard, Janell, 60
I Know Why the Caged Bird Sings, 44-45
Jade Flower Palace, 72-73
Jerome, Judson, 52-53, 60
Joe Turner's Come and Gone, 101-2
Johnson, James Weldon, 15
Knowlt Hoheimer, 5-6, 8
Lee, Dennis, 54
Lee, Harper, 27, 41-42
Livingston, Myra Cohn, 50
Longfellow, Henry Wadsworth, 55, 60
Lover's Toy, A, 60, 65
Lucinda Matlock, 4-5, 8
Lydia Puckett, 5-6, 8
McAfee, Tom, 21-22
McGinley, Phyllis, 55-56
Mansfield, Katherine, 24-25
Masters, Edgar Lee, 4-6, 60
Miller, Arthur, 116-17
Miss Brill, 24-25
My Mother Pieced Quilts, 71-72
My Sister's Marriage, 23
Nelson, Gale, 107
On Saturday Afternoon, 23
Only the Dead Know Brooklyn, 24
Oranges, 67-68
Pirates of Penzance, The, 16

Poe, Edgar Allan, 19-20, 29-39
Porphyria's Lover, 60, 70-71
Rawls, Wilson, 40-41
Rich, Cynthia Marshall, 23
Romeo and Juliet, 59, 97-98
Rose, Reginald, 82, 99-100
Runaway, The, 69
Sandburg, Carl, 53, 60
Sea Gull, 51-52
Shakespeare, William, 59, 97-98
Shapiro, Karl, 61-65
Shaw, Bernard, 103-5
Sillitoe, Alan, 23
Silverstein, Shel, 49
Simon, Neil, 76-86
Soto, Gary, 67-68
This is My Living Room, 21-22, 28

To Kill a Mockingbird, 27, 41-42
Tu Fu, 72-73
Twain, Mark, 23, 27
Ugliest Pilgrim, The, 24
Unicorn, The, 110-12
Voice, The, 107
Warren, Anne, 50
Welty, Eudora, 22-23
We're Racing, Racing Down the Walk, 55-56
When the Legends Die, 45-46
Where the Red Fern Grows, 40-41
Why I Live at the P.O., 22-23
Williams, William Carlos, 57-58
Wilson, August, 101-2
Wolfe, Thomas, 24
Young Lady of Property, A, 105, 113-16

Getting Started in Oral Interpretation